Faith Lessons from an Adoption Attorney's Adventures

ALICE H. MURRAY

Birmingham, Alabama

God Adopted Us First

Iron Stream
An imprint of Iron Stream Media
100 Missionary Ridge
Birmingham, AL 35242
IronStreamMedia.com

Copyright © 2025 by Alice H. Murray

No part of this publication may be reproduced, stored in a retrieval system, or transmitted in any form or by any means—electronic, mechanical, photocopying, recording, or otherwise—without the prior written permission of the publisher.

Iron Stream Media serves its authors as they express their views, which may not express the views of the publisher.

This book reflects the author's present recollections of experiences over time. Some names and characteristics have been changed to protect the privacy of individuals. While the author has taken efforts to ensure the accuracy of the content, there may be mistakes in typography or content, since it was written as a true account of the author. Also, this book provides information only up to the publishing date. Therefore, it should be used as a guide—not as the ultimate source.

Library of Congress Control Number: 2024948940

All Scripture quotations, unless otherwise indicated, are taken from the Holy Bible, New International Version®, NIV®. Copyright ©1973, 1978, 1984, 2011 by Biblica, Inc.™ Used by permission of Zondervan. All rights reserved worldwide. www.zondervan.com The "NIV" and "New International Version" are trademarks registered in the United States Patent and Trademark Office by Biblica, Inc.™

Scripture quotations marked KJV are from The Authorized (King James) Version. Rights in the Authorized Version in the United Kingdom are vested in the Crown. Reproduced by permission of the Crown's patentee, Cambridge University Press

Scripture quotations marked (TLB) are taken from *The Living Bible*, copyright © 1971 by Tyndale House Foundation. Used by permission of Tyndale House Publishers, Carol Stream, Illinois 60188. All rights reserved.

Cover design by twolineSTUDIO.com

ISBN: 978-1-56309-781-2 (paperback)
ISBN: 978-1-56309-782-9 (ebook)

1 2 3 4 5—29 28 27 26 25

If you've ever considered adoption or were adopted or have already adopted children, you will love this beautiful book by Alice Murray. Alice was an adoption attorney for thirty-five years. Now she tells some of the stories about her work and all the many clients she helped through beautiful devotionals powered by Scripture. I laughed and cried through most of these amazing stories that show us God is always in the details. Not only did I find the stories fascinating and heartbreaking, but I also saw joy in many of them. Unexpected joy—the kind only the Lord can make happen.

What a great tribute to God from a true servant who fought the good fight and united so many families with children who needed them. Highly recommend this book. —**Lenora Worth**, *New York Times*, *Publishers Weekly*, and *USA Today* best-selling Christian fiction author and adoptive grandmother

This book hit all the right chords with me. Not only does Alice Murray give us a fascinating glimpse into the world of an adoption attorney, she speaks to the very heart of what it means to be adopted into the family of God. Each true story was so riveting that I probably would have devoured the whole book in one sitting if the faith lessons at the end of the chapters weren't so thought-provoking. As an adoptive parent and former CASA volunteer, I truly appreciate the candor and heart that went into this power-packed devotional, and I can't wait to share it with everyone I know. —**Annette Marie Griffin**, adoptive mother, award-winning writer, author of *What's a Family?*

As an adopted child myself, I have experienced the beauty of adoption. As a Christian, I have received the unconditional love from our heavenly Father. Reading these touching stories from Alice's journey as an adoption attorney reminded me of the truth of both of those experiences! The stories themselves are captivating, but the way she connects each one to a biblical truth is the real takeaway. Whether you are a part of the adoption triad or not, I think you'll find Alice's book to be an inspiring and worthy read! —**Marcia Ramirez**, adoptee, founder and president of God and My Girlfriends Ministries, singer-songwriter, author of *God, My Girlfriends & Me*

Alice H. Murray's book, *God Adopted Us First*, combines devotional exercises with compelling stories from her thirty-five years as an adoption attorney. Throughout her career, she has worked closely with birth mothers, adoptive parents, and others impacted by adoption. This book offers a fresh and engaging perspective from a credible voice in the discussions surrounding adoption, love, loss, law, and faith. —**Rhonda M. Roorda**, adoptee, award-winning author, and adoption consultant (including work for NBC's Emmy Award–winning TV series *This Is Us*)

As someone who is proud to be called "Aunt Michelle" to a very special adopted young man, I have seen the good, bad, and ugly surrounding adoption. That's why I love the honesty in this book. Author Alice Murray shares poignant stories from her work as an attorney in the world of adoption, and she wraps each one in hope and love. Readers will not only gain a greater understanding of adoption—both in the natural and spiritually speaking—but also readers will be challenged in their own faith adventures, learning lessons from each entry. This book is beautifully written and heartfelt, and I will be gifting it to many. —**Michelle Medlock Adams**, *New York Times* best-selling author, including, *Love Connects Us All*, which focuses on expanding families through adoption and foster care

Author Alice Murray powerfully weaves the beauty of earthly adoption with the profound truth of our adoption into God's family. Each reflection draws readers closer to God's heart, reminding us that we are chosen, loved, and redeemed by His grace. It is a beautiful encouragement for anyone seeking to understand God's love more deeply through the lens of adoption. —**Patti Smith**, adoptee, publisher of *GO! Christian Magazine*

As Alice outlines in the introduction, adoption is near and dear to God's heart. Children adopted by Christian families who instill their faith in their children are blessed to be adopted twice. I have witnessed this blessing in my own household and in my work as an adoption professional, and I find this book such a true reflection of that blessing. This collection of adoption stories covers the joys, the trials, and the sometimes humor of the adoption process and ties it with biblical principles. Alice's use of scripture and analytically tying the stories with the same is remarkable and enjoyable. This is such a good read for birth parents, adoptive parents, and adoptees. —**Daniel M. Hartzog Jr.**, Executive Pastor of Appointed Church; Executive Director and attorney for Heartfelt Adoptions and Surrogacy Services, LLC; adoptive father to two amazing daughters

To a special forever family—my sister Dorothy, her husband, Mike, and their two adopted children—who gave me the opportunity to experience the adoption process as a family member in addition to experiencing it as an adoption professional.

Contents

Introduction ix
Adventure 1: A Mother's Gift 1
Adventure 2: Make a Joyful Noise 5
Adventure 3: Denied a Baby 9
Adventure 4: Captain Kangaroo 13
Adventure 5: Nothing More Than Feelings 17
Adventure 6: It's a Secret! 21
Adventure 7: "Where Everybody Knows Your Name" 25
Adventure 8: Come, Thou Long Expected Doctor 29
Adventure 9: Don't Judge a Book by Its Cover 33
Adventure 10: Turning Water into Wine 37
Adventure 11: Unexpected Arrival 41
Adventure 12: And She Shall Be Called 45
Adventure 13: The Black Sheep 49
Adventure 14: Pizza Hut Delivery 53
Adventure 15: For Such a Time as This 57
Adventure 16: The Curve 61
Adventure 17: "I Can't Bear It" 65
Adventure 18: Seeing Evil 69
Adventure 19: "Boss of the Babies" 73

Adventure 20: "I Forgot" 77

Adventure 21: Peer Pressure 81

Adventure 22: All I Want for Christmas.................. 85

Adventure 23: Dressed for Success? 89

Adventure 24: Tom, Dick, or Harry? 93

Adventure 25: Religiously Following the Rules 99

Adventure 26: Will the Real Birth Mother Please Stand Up? . . 105

Adventure 27: Miss Kitty.............................. 109

Adventure 28: "I Had a Dream"......................... 113

Adventure 29: What's in a Name? 117

Adventure 30: It Only Takes Once....................... 121

Adventure 31: "Help! He's Trying to Kill Me!"............. 127

Adventure 32: Disturbing Darkness 131

Adventure 33: "You Ain't Gettin' on This Base!"............ 137

Adventure 34: "Why Are Those People Looking at Me?" 143

Adventure 35: Poker Face.............................. 149

Adventure 36: Spitting Image 155

Adventure 37: Bond, Jane Bond......................... 159

Adventure 38: "Gypsies, Tramps, and Thieves".............. 163

Adventure 39: Asked and Answered 169

Adventure 40: Be Prepared............................. 173

Acknowledgments 179

About the Author.................................... 181

Introduction

Adoption is much like making sausage. Some may not want to hear the real story because it isn't pretty. In fact, it can be very messy.

The truth? Placing a child for adoption is a heartbreaking decision for most birth mothers. For the few who don't care, it's difficult for adoption professionals to witness that lack of love. The circumstances leading to an unplanned pregnancy are not the stuff of Hallmark movies. They may, for example, involve crimes committed against the birth mother. Likewise, adoptive parents suffer, too, grieving the loss of children through miscarriage, stillbirth, and/or the loss of the opportunity to raise a biological child. But despite its messiness, people need to know the truth because it elevates the understanding of both the pain and love involved in adoptions.

Love is adoption's biggest lesson. Adoption teaches about love for a child (ours or someone else's), love to show our fellow man (even those who are considered "bad"), and, most especially, the amount of giving love requires.

What Is Adoption?

Today most people think of adoption as merely a legal process. While, yes, courts and laws are involved in creating a family recognized by the law, adoption is also a clear reflection of God's love for us. Because of that love, God allowed His Son Jesus to be taken from earthly life via a cruel death on a cross so we could become members of His family. How do I know this? Because the Bible tells me so! Read Galatians 4:4–5 and Ephesians 1:5, which discuss our "adoption" to sonship. These passages mean *every Christian is adopted*.

The biblically embraced practice of adoption reminds us of the great sacrifice God made. Jesus gave up His life, but God gave up His Son. Anyone who has seen tears flow down a birth mother's cheeks, heard the heart-wrenching cries she emits, or observed the pain in her eyes when she lets go of her flesh and blood for the child's best interest will hold a new appreciation for Father God's pain. He took on that pain because He loved you and me that much.

Because God is love, Christians are called to love one another. Interestingly, James 1:27 states the purest type of faith involves caring for "orphans." Even if a parent is still alive, a child might be a virtual orphan due to parental circumstances such abandonment, drug addiction, or incarceration. Adoption provides a means for a child to have a permanent, stable, and loving family.

Adoption Stories in the Bible

Sprinkled throughout the Bible are adoption stories involving various types of adoption. Don't believe me? Let's check the Good Book.

Exodus 2 relates that Pharaoh's daughter adopted Moses after his mother placed him in a basket in the Nile's bulrushes to give her son a chance at life. In fact, the Egyptian royal gave the baby the name Moses in reference to her having drawn him out of the water.

God's plan was for Moses to be adopted and raised in court. How else could Moses acquire the education and leadership skills to lead throngs of Israelites through the wilderness? God used Moses to save His people. This Bible story is an example of an interracial adoption as an Egyptian raised a Hebrew. And since no husband of Pharaoh's daughter is mentioned, the adoption may have been one by a single parent.

Queen Esther was not only beautiful but also an adoptee. According to Esther 2:7, Esther's older cousin Mordecai adopted and raised her as his daughter after both of her parents died. God's plan involved Esther being in the palace and "in" with the king. Her presence in the king's life and court allowed her to plead on behalf of her people whom Haman plotted to have slaughtered. God used Esther to save the Jewish people. Her story is an example of a relative adoption.

Jesus had no earthly biological father. Joseph, his stepfather, raised Jesus as his own. The people of Nazareth viewed Jesus as "the carpenter's son" (Matthew 13:55). God uses Jesus to save everyone who accepts the gift of salvation (John 3:16). Jesus's upbringing is an example of a stepparent adoption.

My Adoption Work Journey

Although I never set out to be, nor even considered being, an adoption attorney, it's what God wanted me to do. He orchestrated the circumstances for me to have that kind of legal practice, one I'd never have chosen. Not that I rejected an adoption practice, but the option wasn't one of which I was even aware when I graduated from law school. But then God placed the opportunity right in my lap.

Over three and a half decades, adoption work in Florida took me on crazy adventures and taught me more about my faith. Trust me, I could not handle adoptions without believing in God. Too many "coincidences" happened and miracles occurred. And God's constant presence enabled me to handle the challenging circumstances I faced.

My Writing Journey

Seeing the reflection of God's love in adoption spurred me to write something connecting the dots between that legal process and faith. God taught me numerous faith lessons from my adoption work, and I would be selfish not to share this knowledge and inspiration with others.

Writing about adoption provides me the chance to show the truth about adoption. Aside from love, God is also truth. Most of the time I find that the media, and often the public, portrays adoption inaccurately. Birth mothers who choose adoption for their child are not "giving away their baby." They are acting as a mother should, making sure their child is provided for when they cannot do so. Adoption attorneys are not "baby sellers." That type of practice is illegal, but some will skirt, if not absolutely ignore, the law. They are the few bad apples.

I invite you to come along with me as I recount forty of my adoption adventures and the faith lessons I learned from them. And no, I did not make up any of these situations nor have I dramatized the details. It's just the facts with names changed or not mentioned to respect the privacy of those involved. Read on to learn the truth about adoption, learn about love, learn more about adoption, and most of all, deepen your faith. Remember, God adopted us first.

Adventure 1

A Mother's Gift

A teary-eyed pregnant girl occupied a chair across from me on the other side of my desk. My boss sat next to me in my office as we faced the upset young woman. "But what if my child hates me for placing him for adoption?" she sputtered, unsuccessfully attempting to maintain her composure.

"Let me tell you a story," my boss responded. "I received a call here at the office one day from a young man. The caller started off by saying, 'You probably don't remember me, but you handled my adoption eighteen years ago. I'm calling because I wanted to see if you could put me in touch with my birth mother. I want to thank her for what she has done for me.'"

In the story, the caller went on to say the previous evening he'd been sitting in his bedroom and thinking about his life. He recognized that it had been a wonderful one. His mother had been a full-time mom, and his father had been involved and even coached some of his sports teams.

"I got a great education and have been awarded a scholarship to the college I've always wanted to attend," he stated.

At this point, the young man noted, he felt like he needed to get up and go thank his parents for what they had done for him. "But then," the adoptee explained, "it struck me like a lightning bolt. The person I really needed to thank was my birth mother."

By now, I was struggling to hold back my tears and maintain a professional composure. The pregnant girl reached for a tissue from the box on the corner of my desk and dabbed her eyes as my boss continued the story.

"I recognized," said the adoptee, "that eighteen years ago my birth mother sat in a hospital bed with tears in her eyes as she signed the adoption papers. It was hard for her to do, but what she did by signing those papers was to take my life, wrap it up in gift paper, and hand it to me."

Tears rolled down my cheeks, my boss's voice broke a little, and the young woman shook as she cried. Except for sniffles, silence enveloped the room for a short period. Raw emotion hung in the air.

This heartrending story answered the pregnant girl's concerns. What she heard provided her with the courage to move forward with an adoptive placement. Yes, she knew it would be hard. But a wonderful life, one she knew she was in no position to give, was the gift she desired to give the child she carried and loved.

Faith Lesson

> *For the wages of sin is death, but the gift of God is eternal life in Christ Jesus our Lord.*
>
> —Romans 6:23

Who doesn't like to receive a gift? Usually, we think of gifts as material things placed in a box which is then decorated with attractive wrapping paper, ribbons or bows, and a card. What fun to tear into it and see what we have been given!

But not all gifts are tangible. Clothing and toys can be placed in a box, but a gift might also be an experience. When I was growing up, I always asked to go to an Atlanta Braves baseball game for my birthday. And boy was I happy when my loving dad gave me that present.

Our heavenly Father also gives good gifts to His children. But we don't receive them in the mail, and we don't unwrap them. They are usually intangible. He gave us the beauty of the world He created for us to live in. He gave us life. He may give us health. But since these gifts aren't concrete and don't come in flashy packages, we often overlook them and fail to thank Him for them.

The Bible tells us that "every good and perfect gift is from above" (James 1:17). But of all the gifts God's children receive from Him, one stands head and shoulders above the rest. Like the birth mother who gave her son a wonderful future, God also gives His children a good life to look forward to. While earthly life will end at some point, God has gifted those who receive His Son with eternal life. Now that's the best gift that could ever be given!

Lesson Learned: Our heavenly Father's gift to us is eternal life.

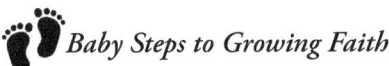 *Baby Steps to Growing Faith*

1. Do you only take note of gifts from God that are tangible, such as an unexpected check received in a time of financial need?

2. List four gifts from God for which you can be thankful.

3. What gift has God given you *today*?

4. Why is eternal life a *gift* from God?

Adventure 2

Make a Joyful Noise

The day began like all days at the office, filled with the usual paper pushing. Then the phone rang.

The receptionist informed me a hospital social worker from another county was calling. After grabbing the phone to speak with her, I learned a baby had just been born at that facility. The child's mother informed the staff she wanted to make an adoptive placement. Unfortunately, no adoption plan was in place. So much for a normal day at the office.

With the receipt of this news, it was off to the races. I called the birth mother, who instructed me to simply pick the "best couple" to receive her child. She left the determination of "best" up to our office, a responsibility I took seriously.

While our office kept files on numerous wonderful couples, the challenge was locating an adoptive couple able to take placement of the baby within the next twenty-four to forty-eight hours upon his discharge from the hospital. After reviewing files of prospective adoptive couples, my boss and I agreed on a lovely, childless young couple who were already approved for a placement. Would they be interested and able to receive a baby with little notice?

Given it was the middle of a business day and time was of the essence, I had no choice but to call the prospective adoptive mother at her work. She was a pharmacist, but she dropped everything she was doing to take my call. Informing her about the last-minute opportunity, I told her this placement was theirs if she and her husband wanted to accept it.

The response? A piercing scream followed by weeping. Through tears, the prospective adoptive mother answered in the affirmative. Sheepishly, she then told me her customers and some other employees were looking at her in concern. The emotional woman requested I hold as she conveyed the exciting news to them. Over the phone I heard clapping and cheers from those in the pharmacy. What a joyful noise she and all those present with her made at this life-changing moment.

Faith Lesson

> *Make a joyful noise unto the LORD, all ye lands.*
> —Psalm 100:1 KJV

The word *noise* typically has a negative connotation. We think of loud music coming from a neighbor's house or perhaps the sound of construction work in the area. We'd prefer the sound of silence, please.

But when it comes to gifts given to us by others, our silence is offensive. The gift giver wants to know the present offered is pleasing and appreciates hearing words of gratitude. An excited "Thank you!" or "It's just what I wanted!" warms the giver's heart.

How many times have we received gifts from our heavenly Father? Aren't they received daily? We experience another day of life, the love of family, the guiding of the Holy Spirit. But do we make a joyful noise to express how we feel? The Scriptures urge interaction with the Lord, making clear the joy He's allowed in our lives and our gratitude for it. Go on, make a joyful noise!

Lesson Learned: Expressions of gratitude are a joyful noise God loves to hear.

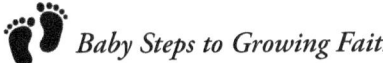 *Baby Steps to Growing Faith*

1. How does a verbal expression of gratitude, whether words or sounds (squeals, hand clapping, and so on), make you feel when you give a gift?

2. What does silence on the part of a gift recipient convey to you?

3. How can you make a joyful noise unto the Lord?

4. When should you make a joyful noise unto the Lord?

Adventure 3

Denied a Baby

Choosing an adoptive placement for her child isn't the end of the birth mother's decision-making. Many more issues must be settled. Does she want to see the baby following birth? Does she want to name the child? Does she want the prospective adoptive couple to be at the hospital for the birth? *Wait.* Who will be adopting her child? That question is her biggest decision to make after selecting the adoption option.

What do birth mothers want in a couple? The specifications vary widely depending on the desires of each woman, who is, in the end, a unique individual. Common requests include that the couple be nonsmokers, have a pet, or be affiliated with a specific religion or denomination.

One birth mother quickly responded to my query as to what she desired for potential adoptive parents. She requested a particular Christian denomination. Such an affiliation was a firm requirement, not simply that she'd like them to be that denomination if possible.

The denomination was not one of the most common, so a certain couple immediately came to mind. They had listed this denomination as their religious affiliation on the intake form. This husband and wife were in their early forties, secure in their careers, and impressed me during our first meeting. Their desire to adopt was a strong one. Given their age, they realized time was a factor for them to receive a placement before they got "too old" to parent a newborn.

I called the wife and explained the basic details of the birth mother's situation. Then I mentioned what she wanted in a family. A long pause followed. Finally, the wife spoke in a voice she was clearly trying to keep under control.

"You know how much we want to adopt a baby," she began. "But I have to tell you the truth. In the past few months, my husband and I began attending a different church denomination of which we are now members. It is not that denomination. While it would be easy to say we are members of the denomination the birth mother desires, that would not be the truth. I must be honest and pass on this opportunity."

Her response left me speechless. Despite the opportunity to receive her heart's desire, this woman denied herself that chance by putting her faith into practice and not lying. She did the right thing, but surely her heart was breaking. She displayed integrity and lived out her beliefs, but her arms were left achingly empty.

How many people in the same position would have made this choice? I still reflect on her decision to this day.

Faith Lesson

> *Then he said to them all: "Whoever wants to be my disciple must deny themselves and take up their cross daily and follow me."*

—Luke 9:23

Anyone who believes a Christian's faith walk is all wine and roses is sadly mistaken. Accepting Jesus as our Savior does not mean life becomes a cakewalk. In fact, the opposite is true. The Christian life is an ongoing difficult journey.

Jesus provided truth in advertising. He transparently told His listeners what following Him entailed. Being His disciple would require much of someone, and it would be a struggle.

Specifically, Jesus noted that self-denial is part of being a Christian. We can't have all the things we want. Why? Because some desires are sinful and at odds with the essence of being a Christian. Being self-indulgent by giving in to sexual temptation or material wants puts us on the throne rather than God. Other desires might require us to commit a sin, such as lying or stealing, to obtain what we want.

Self-denial isn't a onetime thing either. It is a daily practice according to Jesus, and it won't be easy. The extent of self-denial's difficulty is conveyed by His comment that we must take up our cross. Historians estimate a typical Roman cross likely weighed over three hundred pounds.[1] Now that's heavy!

While we may not literally have to carry a heavy cross in our faith walk, we will face heavy burdens. As this honest prospective adoptive mother illustrated, sometimes the burden is a heavy heart.

Lesson Learned: Following Jesus requires denial of self.

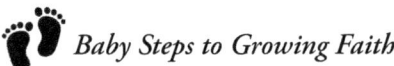
Baby Steps to Growing Faith

1. Identify a time in your own faith life when self-denial was the appropriate action.

---

1 "What Is the Weight of the Cross That Jesus Carried?" *Biblword*, March 14, 2022, https://www.biblword.net/what-is-the-weight-of-the-cross-that-jesus-carried/.

2. If you don't deny yourself in the face of temptation, who is #1 in your life at that point?

3. Why did Jesus say His disciples must *daily* take up their crosses?

4. How do you respond to an unbeliever who rejects Christianity because living out the faith would require self-denial?

Adventure 4

Captain Kangaroo

For most people, going to court is an out of the ordinary and scary experience. They have no idea what to expect in the courtroom other than what they've seen on some TV legal drama. To be honest, those shows aim for entertainment and do not always jibe with existing legal rules. They rarely, if ever, depict what happens in an adoption final hearing.

To help combat this fear of the unknown, I explain to clients in advance what will happen when we get to the courtroom. I tell them how long the hearing might take, who'll be present, and other tidbits to make them feel more comfortable about what they are facing.

One day I sat in our office's lobby talking with a prospective adoptive couple just before going to court. Since the judge's presence in a robe on his raised bench is often intimidating, I sought to alleviate fear of the man in charge of the courtroom.

"The judge we're appearing before is a very nice man," I told my clients. "He loves final adoption hearings because everyone will leave his courtroom happy. If there are any tears," I joked, "they'll merely be tears of joy."

To drive the point home, I described the judge. "He looks just like Captain Kangaroo in the old kids' TV show." The Captain was a jovial man with white hair who radiated warmth to viewers.

Unfortunately, I did it to myself. In attempting to make sure my clients had a good experience in the courtroom, I set myself up for a disconcerting moment. When the judge entered the courtroom and took his seat, he announced, "Ms. Murray, I've reviewed the file, and everything is in order. I don't need to hear any testimony. However, I know this is a big day for your clients, and I'm happy to hear anything they may have to say."

Obligingly, I turned from the podium where I stood before the judge to the table behind me where my clients sat. They looked at me, looked at each other, and then looked back at me. The husband, apparently chosen to speak on behalf of the couple, addressed the judge.

"Our attorney is right, your Honor," he said matter-of-factly. "You do look like Captain Kangaroo." That was it. He said nothing more.

The beloved kids' TV show character, Captain Kangaroo.

I was mortified and wished the floor would open to swallow me. When my wish wasn't granted, I sheepishly turned to the judge and explained that in attempting to reduce the clients' anxiety about coming to court, I had likened him to a kid-friendly, fictional character.

To my relief, the judge smiled. He then said, "That's all right, Ms. Murray. This isn't the first time I've been compared to Captain Kangaroo." He explained that his buddies from his military days called him "Captain" for that very reason.

Whew! Who'd want a judge you regularly appeared before having it out for you because you described him in a way he didn't like? While I don't remember the clients' names, the gender or age of the child they were adopting, or the day of the week the hearing occurred, I'll never forget that awkward moment in "Captain Kangaroo's" court.

Faith Lesson

> *But I tell you that everyone will have to give account on the day of judgment for every empty word they have spoken.*
>
> —Matthew 12:36

A familiar adage tells us to think before speaking. Why? Because once words are spoken, they cannot be taken back. It will be too late to think about what you should have said.

Unfortunately, we are more likely to simply blurt out the first thing that comes to mind rather than taking time to consider our reply. But words matter. They can cause hurt if spoken in anger. They can fail to help if not properly thought out. They can be a missed opportunity to show kindness or share our faith.

After some carelessly spoken words leave our lips, we may dismiss them as an "error in judgment." Unfortunately, whatever we say or do will ultimately be reviewed by a judge. And that judge will be the Almighty Himself. Forget being nervous appearing before an earthly judge in a courtroom. All of us will eventually appear before the ultimate judge, God, the creator of the universe. Yes, God is a loving heavenly Father, but he cannot tolerate sin. He will not laugh off our regrettable words or actions.

Lesson Learned: One day, we all will stand before the ultimate judge and be called to account for our words and actions.

 Baby Steps to Growing Faith

1. Describe a time when something you said came back to bite you.

2. How does it make you feel to know that one day you will be called to account to God for your words and actions?

3. A punch can hurt the victim physically, but how can words hurt a person?

4. Read John 1:14. If Jesus is referred to as "the Word," does that change your view of how important words can be?

Adventure 5

Nothing More Than Feelings

While there is only one birth mother involved in an adoption, it's possible to have more than one father. That's because the law recognizes different types of fathers. A man who contributes sperm to conceive a baby is a biological father. However, a man who is married to the mother when she conceives or when she gives birth is the child's legal father. This legal relationship exists whether the husband is the child's biological father or not and springs from the law's presuming legitimacy when a married woman bears a child.

Because the concept of a legal father exists, it is not sufficient to ask a woman seeking to place her child for adoption merely who the baby's father is. Of course, she is asked to identify the biological father. But the inquiry does not stop there. An adoption professional must find out if the woman has ever been married and, if so, when. Should she have been married when she got pregnant or when she delivered the child sought to be adopted, a legal father exists and must be contacted about the adoption under Florida law.

In one case, the intake form indicated the birth mother was unmarried at the time of her child's conception and birth. Those facts meant no legal father existed whom we were required to contact for the case. Good. The adoption appeared straightforward.

After securing the necessary consents for the adoption, the Petition For Adoption had to be prepared and filed with the court. A staff member began to gather the documentation routinely submitted to the court along with the petition, including the marriage record for the adopting couple and the birth certificate for the child to be adopted.

Shockingly, the birth certificate revealed the father listed was the birth mother's husband. And he was *not* the biological father who had signed a consent. What? Rechecking the intake form, the paralegal confirmed the birth mother had stated she had not been married when the child was born. This discrepancy called for clarification.

A staff member called the birth mother, explaining that the child's birth certificate showed the birth mother was married when her child was born. This information, however, conflicted with the intake form stating she was unmarried at both her child's conception and birth. Would she please explain?

The explanation given was a head-scratching one. According to the birth mother, she and her husband were separated when she became pregnant by someone else. Because of the length of the separation from her husband, the birth mother said, "I didn't feel married." So she told our office she wasn't.

She may not have felt married, but in the eyes of the law, the birth mother was legally married. Facts trumped feelings and dealing with the legal father in the case was necessary, thus delaying the adoption's finalization.

Faith Lesson

> *Not every one that saith unto me, Lord, Lord, shall enter into the kingdom of heaven; but he that doeth the will of my Father which is in heaven.*
>
> —Matthew 7:21 KJV

Truth is absolute. It does not depend on our feelings. We may not "feel" old, but the age indicated by the date of birth on our driver's license indicates otherwise. We may not "feel" overweight, but the number showing on our bathroom scale belies that feeling.

Feelings can lead believers down the wrong path in their faith life. We might feel "unworthy" before God due to our past behaviors and actions, but Jesus's blood has turned our record white as snow in our Father's eyes. How we feel is not a gauge of the truth of our redemption.

Feelings can also lead nonbelievers down the path to destruction. Often, people feel they are saved because they have been "good" people; their actions are certainly sufficient to give them a stamp of approval in God's eyes. But this feeling is wrong. The truth is that only one way leads to eternal life—salvation provided by accepting Jesus. *Feeling* saved has nothing to do with it.

Lesson Learned: How we feel is not a gauge of the truth.

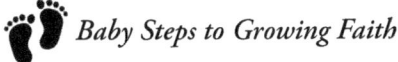
Baby Steps to Growing Faith

1. Do you have to "feel" something for it to be true?

2. Do feelings have a proper place in your faith? If so, where is it?

3. How reliable are feelings? Read Jeremiah 17:9.

4. Do feelings change over time? Does God's truth?

Adventure 6

It's a Secret!

Given the number of military installations in the Florida Panhandle, interactions with active-duty members were commonplace in my practice. What was not common, though, was one military member's secret mission—an adoptive placement of the baby she was expecting but the military didn't know about.

While it is not unusual for a female troop to become pregnant, the circumstances of this situation could easily have been a soap opera plot. Both the birth mother and the birth father were active-duty military. How did they know each other? The birth father just so happened to be the birth mother's supervisor, a man in a position of authority over her. Let's just say this type of situation is frowned upon by the military and not allowed for obvious reasons.

But rules are made to be broken, and the birth father proceeded to do so. To his shock, and likely horror, the birth mother became pregnant because of his rule breaking. Having the military learn of this pregnancy resulting from a prohibited relationship would be catastrophic for the birth father's military career. The birth mother, while not willing to have an abortion, told the man she wanted to carry the baby and place the child for adoption. What choice did the birth father have?

This plan had a few obstacles to be overcome though. The birth mother was on deployment status and required to report a pregnancy. She made no such report and hid her condition. She also failed to go to required periodic physical examinations because, of course, her pregnancy would have been detected. Apparently, the military was too busy keeping its eyes on the enemy to know what was going on with its own troops because it was unaware of her condition or that she was missing required medical appointments.

The second obstacle to hurdle? The birth mother's growing belly. How could she hide her baby bump while in uniform? Fortunately, BDU's (battle dress uniforms) are quite roomy. Plus, the material from which they are made aims to camouflage the wearer. Mission accomplished!

Delivery arrangement posed the biggest problem. The military would find out about the forbidden relationship leading to the pregnancy if she gave birth in the base hospital. The solution? Deliver the baby off base. But how would that cost be covered if medical care was provided by the military? Time for the birth father to step up to the plate. He "generously" offered to pay the expense for delivery at a civilian hospital out of his own pocket—to save his own career of course.

But as a military member, the birth mother couldn't simply take a day off to have a baby whenever the need arose. No sweat. The birth mother had leave built up. She requested and received approval for two weeks off around her due date. Thus, her absence from her duty station raised no suspicions.

The plan failed right? Who could keep a secret that big from the mighty US military? Surprise! The plan worked. The birth mother placed her baby for adoption from the hospital, recovered from delivery during the balance of her leave, and returned to work on base without a baby bump or a baby.

Faith Lesson

> *For God will bring every deed into judgment,*
> *including every hidden thing,*
> *whether it is good or evil.*
>
> —Ecclesiastes 12:14

Can you keep a secret? Perhaps you can keep one from your family, your friends, your employer, or even the United States government. It may take self-discipline, planning, and possibly even outright lies, but it can be done. People can, and do, keep secrets, and they get away with things they have done.

But there's someone you can never keep a secret from—God. The Creator of the universe is not only all-powerful, but He is also all-knowing. He is aware of what you do not only in public but also in secret. The US military may be ignorant of the adoption story I have told, but He is not.

God is not only aware of our actions, but He will ultimately judge them. People on earth may avoid being held accountable for what they have done in this life. But that result will never happen with God. A judgment day will come, and those deeds will be revealed and reviewed. With God, there will always be accountability.

Lesson Learned: We may be able to hide things from other people, but God sees and will judge hidden things.

Baby Steps to Growing Faith

1. Identify a time you have tried to keep a secret from someone. Were you successful?

2. What was the result when a secret you tried to keep from someone was revealed?

3. How does it affect your thinking to know God is aware of all our actions, even those no one else knows about?

4. Does keeping a secret make a situation worse?

Adventure 7

"Where Everybody Knows Your Name"

Florida law dictates *how* a consent must be signed—before a notary and two witnesses—but does not say *where* a consent should be signed. A hospital room typically serves as the signing location when a newborn is being placed for adoption upon discharge. Nevertheless, I have handled the signing of this life-changing paperwork in some unexpected locations as well.

Sometimes signing a consent outside the hospital arises out of necessity. For example, in one case, the birth mother gave birth at a hospital but wanted to leave the facility as soon as possible. Since the hospital was an hour and a half drive from my office, I couldn't get there before she was ready to fly the coop.

No worries, though. The birth mother headed home to the apartment she shared with the birth father. Since I would serve as the notary, that part was covered. We just needed the two witnesses. She assured me her next-door neighbors would be happy to serve as the two required witnesses for signing the adoption paperwork.

But the best laid plans, of course, often go awry. The next-door neighbors weren't home, and neither was anyone else the birth parents knew in the small apartment complex. I was too far away from the office to send for staff members to come serve as witnesses for me.

Then the birth father came up with a solution. Why not go to their place of employment? Coworkers could serve as witnesses for the paperwork. My concern? The birth parents worked in a bar, a quite unusual public location for signing confidential legal paperwork. But the suggested site was the best option under the circumstances, so off we went to the local watering hole.

Arriving at the bar, the three of us entered together. Like in the TV show *Cheers*, shouts of their names greeted them. At least it was a friendly environment.

We took seats at a round table in the middle of the bar. So much for privacy while signing important documents. A waitress came over and asked if we wanted a drink. The birth father immediately placed an order for an alcoholic beverage, while the birth mother and I declined.

I sighed under my breath. The birth father's drink order meant I could not take his consent then. Signing important legal paperwork after consuming alcohol is a big no-no. Why? Alcohol can impair a person's judgment, and the birth father's drinking it then might call into question the validity of the consent he signed. He would need to sign the paperwork at a later point when claims of possible impairment couldn't be raised.

So I turned my attention to the birth mother. The signing of her consent went smoothly, and I left the bar alone after we were done. No one yelled goodbye. Apparently, I hadn't been in the establishment long enough for anyone other than the birth parents to know my name.

Faith Lesson

> *And even the very hairs of your head are all numbered.*
> —Matthew 10:30

The United Nations estimated Planet Earth's population stood at 8,121,911,901 as of July 17, 2024.[2] That number grows daily, of course, with some 385,000 babies born each day around the world.[3] Given those mind-boggling numbers, we can easily feel we are merely an insignificant speck.

A sense of significance is felt, however, when others not only recognize us but also know our name. We feel connected and that we belong when our name is spoken. This truth was evidenced by the birth parents' positive response to hearing their names shouted by coworkers upon entering the bar. Being called by name adds dimension to human relationships.

An awareness of what God knows of us should deepen our relationship with Him. Our heavenly Father not only knows our name, but He knows everything about us. Matthew notes in his Gospel that God does not have a superficial recognition of us. It's not just our name He can voice. He understands the most intimate details about us, even down to the number of hairs on our head.

Our name being shouted in welcome by acquaintances in a bar indicates a superficial connection. Our name, and every other detail about us, being known by the Lord of Lords shows His deep

---

[2] Real-Time World Population Counter Live, WorldPopulation.Live, accessed August 15, 2024, https://worldpopulation.live/.

[3] "How Many Babies Are Born Each Day?" The World Counts, accessed August 15, 2024, https://www.theworldcounts.com/stories/how-many-babies-are-born-each-day.

connection to us and how much He loves and cares about us. How much is that? We are His family members, the children of God through faith in Jesus Christ (Galatians 3:26).

Lesson Learned: God knows *all* about us—not just our name.

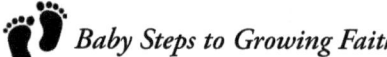 *Baby Steps to Growing Faith*

1. How do you feel when someone greets you by name?

2. How deep is your relationship with someone who knows your name but little else about you?

3. Is your view of your relationship with God altered by awareness that the Creator of the universe knows you intimately—by name and myriad other details about you?

4. God knows your name. By what name do you address Him?

Adventure 8

Come, Thou Long Expected Doctor

Many places offer a fun and entertaining location to spend time on Christmas Eve. Choices include a mall for shopping, a restaurant to gather with friends, and a kitchen to enjoy baking Christmas cookies with grandkids. A hospital is not one of these places. But that's where I spent several long hours one Christmas Eve waiting to get a baby discharged.

Babies, of course, do not respect working hours, the weekend, or holidays. As a result, it wasn't uncommon for me to get a consent signed or make a baby placement during times when I should have been off work. But assisting in the creation of a forever family provides a wonderful incentive to work on a Saturday, at night, and yes, even on holidays.

Such was the case one December. The day I was legally authorized to take a birth mother's consent fell on Christmas Eve due to the waiting period Florida law imposed for signing following her baby's birth. Adding to the inconvenience, the hospital was in a town one and a half hours away from the office.

Misery loves company. My husband and a staff member commiserated with me as I dragged them along to serve as the two required witnesses for the consent signing. By leaving early in the morning, we'd likely be back by midday, giving each of us the afternoon to take care of last-minute Christmas tasks and attend a Christmas Eve service at church. That was the plan anyway.

The holiday assignment got off to a smooth start. The birth mother was ready for us, and her consent and other adoption paperwork were signed in short order by nine a.m. All that remained was getting the baby discharged and picking up the necessary medical records to be filed with the court. These were quick and routine steps compared to getting signatures on a stack of adoption paperwork.

But at this point, my progress hit a brick wall. The attending pediatrician required to sign the baby's discharge order wasn't at the hospital yet. Because it was Christmas Eve, his normal schedule of rounds before office hours didn't apply. So when would he be there? Oh, probably in an hour or two, the nursing staff advised me.

We had no choice but to sit tight. And I mean literally sit. The witnesses and I remained in the hospital room awaiting the doctor's arrival. We took turns sitting on the less-than-comfortable hospital bed and passed the time chatting. And chatting. And chatting.

Lunchtime came and went with no sign of or update on the doctor. Our impatience grew as our stomachs started to rumble. At that point we were afraid to leave to grab a bite because certainly the pediatrician would show up as soon as we left. He had to arrive sometime, and we were confident the nursing staff knew the pediatrician would come.

After six hours of waiting for him, the pediatrician made his much-anticipated appearance around three p.m. Within minutes of his arrival, the discharge order was signed, I had medical records in hand, the adoptive mother had departed the facility with the baby, and the witnesses and I were making a beeline to my car to head to Wendy's for a very late lunch before driving an hour and a half back home. Thankfully the fast food really was *fast* because the doctor had been as slow as Christmas in arriving at the hospital.

Faith Lesson

> *Abraham fell facedown; he laughed and said to himself,*
> *"Will a son be born to a man a hundred years old? Will*
> *Sarah bear a child at the age of ninety?"*
>
> —Genesis 17:17

Time takes on added importance when only a finite amount of it exists. Abraham and his wife, Sarah, were not getting any younger. God had promised them an heir, but no child had been born, and they were up there in years. Ultimately, a quarter of a century passed between the time God initially made this promise and the birth of the couple's son, Isaac. But God had promised something, and He followed through in His perfect timing.

God's timing, though, isn't necessarily our timing. Abraham and Sarah no doubt wanted to have a child soon after God's promise was made. Similarly, as I waited at the hospital on Christmas Eve, I had a fast-food mentality. I wanted the doctor to appear right away.

Instead of concern about the timing, whether of the appearance of a doctor or the blessing of an heir, perhaps we should focus on the certainty of the representation. The hospital staff knew what the doctor's schedule was and that he would be in that day. I could rely on this knowledge for assurance that the doctor would indeed come to the hospital at some point. And God is truth. If He says He will provide an heir or whatever promise He makes, can't we trust His words even if the fulfillment is "delayed" from our perspective?

Lesson Learned: Everything is accomplished in God's time.

 Baby Steps to Growing Faith

1. Has there been an instance in your life when you had to wait a long time for a promise of God's to be fulfilled? If so, did the length of time affect your belief He would keep His promise?

2. How long did God's chosen people have to wait for the appearance of the promised Messiah?

3. Does waiting for a promise of God's to be fulfilled teach patience? Is patience a valuable characteristic in your faith life?

4. What should we do as we wait for fulfillment of a promise by God?

Adventure 9

Don't Judge a Book by Its Cover

Determining where a baby will be placed for adoption is a heavy responsibility. The forever home selected shapes the child's future. So the direction of the child's life rests in an adoption professional's hands.

The law sets certain minimum standards for prospective adoptive parents. They must be financially capable of caring for a child. They cannot have a criminal record containing an offense that would endanger a child's welfare. Their physical home has to offer a safe environment for a child. And then there are *my* requirements. As a mother, in addition to being an adoption attorney, I must be personally satisfied the potential home is one in which I would place my own child.

How can I determine if a couple passes muster for this huge assignment? One-on-one contact is essential. Preferably, I meet with the couple in person for a couple of hours in my office. Carrying on a face-to-face conversation reveals much about an individual, their priorities, and their commitment to assuming child-rearing obligations. Facts on a piece of paper are informative, but my gut is invaluable in evaluating applications from hopeful parents.

But, at the end of the day, I am human. I am not perfect when it comes to assessing others. How do I fail? In one crash-and-burn instance, I did what I wasn't supposed to do and made a judgment based solely on the outside—the couple's physical appearance.

Our office exterior was less important than the work done inside.

From my office window I spotted a couple walking up the sidewalk to our office's front door. *Oh yes, that must be the couple who is here for the adoption consultation with me.*

But looking closer, my spirits fell. *Oh no! This consultation will be such a waste of time.* The man wore a T-shirt, cut-off jean shorts, and sandals. His wife was similarly dressed. *They aren't going to be able to afford an adoption*, I concluded.

My first impression turned 180 degrees, however, once the couple was seated in my office. The two were well educated, licensed professionals with a six-figure income. They had driven over an hour to meet me on a rare day off and had handled other errands on the way to my office, which explained their casual attire.

Best of all, the husband and wife were two of the sweetest people I'd ever met. Their strong Christian faith was evident in their demeanor and interactions with me. My time with them left me with no doubt that they would be a blessing to a baby in need of a forever home.

Embarrassed by the conclusions I'd leapt to prior to the couple entering my office, I took a few minutes after they left to consider where I had gone so wrong. My mother's voice spoke clearly in my head, "Don't judge a book by its cover." That was a mistake I vowed not to repeat in the future—in the office or anywhere else.

Faith Lesson

> *When they arrived, Samuel saw Eliab and thought, "Surely the LORD's anointed stands here before the LORD."*
>
> *But the LORD said to Samuel, "Do not consider his appearance or his height, for I have rejected him. The LORD does not look at the things people look at. People look at the outward appearance, but the LORD looks at the heart."*
>
> —1 Samuel 16:6–7

It's hard not to be taken in by someone's outer appearance. I mean, on what else does a human have to base their first impression? We see how another person presents themselves and how they dress. Don't those things matter?

Samuel, on a mission from God to anoint a king, was just as human as the rest of us. What did he notice when Jesse's sons appeared before him? Hmm. Eliab looked like king material based on his height and physical appearance. Nope. God made clear the outward appearance was a human standard, not His divine one.

What did God look at then? His concern was the future king's heart, something God was in a unique position to see. He took note of the love and concern David had while caring for the sheep. To Him, David wasn't a common, stinky shepherd. Instead, he was the perfect candidate to lead and care for God's sheep. It was the inside, not the outside, that mattered to God then and still does today.

Lesson Learned: It's what's on the inside that is important to God.

 Baby Steps to Growing Faith

1. To your knowledge, has anyone made a snap judgment about you based on something external such as your age, gender, or dress?

2. What does God care about more, how fabulous our wardrobe is or the internal thoughts we have about Him and others?

3. If we are to imitate our heavenly Father, what things should we be looking at in others?

4. What might your first impression have been of an itinerant teacher with roughened hands, common clothing, and few material possessions?

Adventure 10

Turning Water into Wine

Having a woman sign a consent to her newborn's adoption isn't just signing legal documents. It can be a heart-wrenching event. With hormones surging after delivery, the birth mother's emotions are heightened. Crying is common and understandable as she takes pen in hand for this life-altering step. The event is also an emotional roller-coaster ride for everyone else in the room.

Over the years, I developed techniques to cope with the tense atmosphere when a consent is signed. I've learned to go into "attorney mode" where I don't allow emotions to overtake me. If I didn't, I'd dissolve into tears like I do over sappy commercials on TV.

Reducing tension is helpful for birth mothers. Humor helps. Not that signing a consent is funny, but being able to laugh during a difficult time can do the soul good.

A simple humorous remark worked wonders in one memorable case. This birth mother received strong emotional support from the birth father. He stayed with her in the hospital, and the two were in total agreement that an adoptive placement was best for their child under the circumstances. But having them both in the room meant each could sense the sorrow and grief the other was experiencing in addition to their own. It was tough for them and tough for me to watch their emotional struggles.

At some point, the tension reached a peak. The birth mother remarked, "I need a drink." Solicitously, I asked her if I could get her some water. Her response? "Actually, I meant a *drink*, as in alcohol."

Sensing her reaching the brink of not being able to hold it together, I replied in the lightest tone I could, "Well, I don't have any alcohol, but I could get you some water, which you could pretend was white wine."

The young woman gave me a weak smile, but I could sense a bit of emotional release from her. We continued with the paperwork and avoided a waterfall of tears or any type of meltdown.

When we were through, I asked the birth mother if I could do anything else for her. Shaking her head no, she told me how thankful she was with how I had handled doing the paperwork with her. She explained that signing those documents was one of the hardest things she'd ever done. And she noted that a bit of humor had helped her to get through it.

While my remark may not have been all that funny, its humor was the best emotional medicine for a hurting heart at the time. I couldn't turn water into wine, but I did turn a difficult situation into something more bearable. And the true miracle? The young woman's courage allowed a couple's dream of becoming parents to come true.

Faith Lesson

> *Jesus said to the servants, "Fill the jars with water"; so they filled them to the brim.*

> *Then he told them, "Now draw some out and take it to the master of the banquet."*
>
> *They did so, and the master of the banquet tasted the water that had been turned into wine.*
>
> —John 2:7–9

Miracles often involve turning something into something else. Jesus converted a raging sea into calm waters. He made a boy's lunch basket a sufficient meal for thousands. Jesus turned physically ravaged lepers into healed men. And to start His ministry of miracles, He turned jars of water into wine.

The key point in Jesus's miracles is that the result was totally different than what He started with. This achievement underscores God's role as Creator. Our whole world came into being when God spoke and brought life out of nothingness. But God wasn't done with creating just yet. He also created a way for sinful humans to receive eternal life through the provision of His Son as an atoning sacrifice.

Our divine Father is the ultimate creator. Better than water being turned into fruit of the vine? God provided the Living Water to allow man to become a new creature through Him.

Lesson Learned: God is the ultimate Creator.

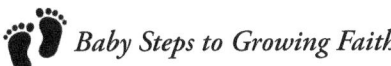

Baby Steps to Growing Faith

1. How do you define a miracle?

2. Has God ever worked a miracle in your life or the life of someone you know?

3. Other than those mentioned above, name three miracles Jesus performed.

4. What purpose do miracles serve?

Adventure 11

Unexpected Arrival

Where do adoption attorneys hang out? Logically attorneys would frequent courthouses. While I spent my share of time in courtrooms handling hearings related to adoption, my work required spending a good bit of time at the hospital as well. Why else would ten or so hospitals appear on my cell phone's contact list?

I appeared at hospitals on a regular basis. Why? Birth mothers typically signed consents for newborn adoptions with me while hospitalized following delivery. Then, in-person arrangements had to be made with the medical staff for babies to be legally discharged to someone other than their biological parent—typically me.

The bottom line is that I was a familiar figure on the maternity floor and in the newborn nursery at several hospitals. While everyone at the bar in *Cheers* knew Norm's name, the nurses at various medical facilities knew mine.

How identified I was with adoptive placements became clear when I traveled to a hospital for personal reasons one day. A female family member had given birth to her first child, so my husband and I made the hour's trip to this hospital to visit. My job made things easy as pie for us. I knew the travel route, where to park, which hospital entrance to use, and which floor to go to see a maternity patient.

Arriving on the maternity floor, I led the way in the direction of our relative's hospital room. This route took us by the nurses' station. I recognized the one nurse manning it. Rather than a welcoming smile or wave from her, I noticed a look of panic.

"Oh! I didn't know you were coming. No one told me there was an adoptive placement, and I don't have any paperwork for you," she rattled off in distress. A second nurse appeared on the scene at that point. Before I could speak, the first nurse asked this coworker if she knew about an adoptive placement. Both began nervously looking through stacks of charts and papers fearing they'd overlooked something.

I gave the nurses a friendly smile and explained I hadn't come for an adoption. Instead, simply visiting a relative was the reason for my presence. Tension rolled off the two women. One laughed and commented that she'd never seen me there except on baby business. "Yes, I do have my own life," I joked.

Relieved, the nurses returned to their duties, and I proceeded to pay a social call on the new mom. But the incident did give me pause. I was inextricably linked to baby placements. How wonderful to be viewed as a stork!

Faith Lesson

So you also must be ready, because the Son of Man will come at an hour when you do not expect him.

—Matthew 24:44

Knowing something is going to happen and being prepared for it when it happens are two very different things. Head knowledge must be supported by some type of action for us to be ready.

When guests come to visit, we have a general, but not necessarily exact, awareness of their arrival time. But knowing they are coming spurs us to undertake appropriate preparations. We clean our houses and make sure we are presentable and ready to entertain the anticipated guests. Simply acknowledging the guests' impending arrival and then going about our business as usual does not make us prepared to welcome them.

The same is true when it comes to Jesus. Are our sins confessed and our hearts clean? Are our current thoughts and actions ones He will find acceptable when we meet face-to-face? Do we even have an idea about what He expects from us that's been gleaned from Bible study? Answering no to any of these questions means we aren't as ready for Jesus's return as we might think.

Annoyance and frustration may occur when medical staff aren't prepared for my arrival at the hospital in an adoption case. But far worse consequences will occur when people aren't prepared for Jesus's second coming. He's made clear He will return. What's not clear? Whether His followers will be ready at that time, which is known only to the Father (Matthew 24:36).

Lesson Learned: Believers must be prepared for Jesus's unknown time of return.

Baby Steps to Growing Faith

1. In what way, if any, do you live your life as if Jesus could return at any time?

2. Other than accepting Jesus as your Savior, how can you prepare for His return?

3. What would you do differently if you knew the exact time of Jesus's return?

4. If our being prepared for Jesus's return is important to Him, why do we give it so little thought?

Adventure 12

And She Shall Be Called

Besides setting up a nursery and buying baby clothes, couples expecting the addition of an infant to the family must select a name for their new family member. Usually, the surname is a no-brainer, but dissension and indecision may arise when it comes to choosing a first and a middle name. So much must be considered—family heritage, beloved family members, avoiding names of ex-boyfriends or girlfriends, what's trendy, and so on.

One couple had no difficulty whatsoever when it came to naming their daughter. This couple was in their early forties and had been married for several years, so they'd had plenty of time to talk about possible names to bestow on a female offspring. They had decided they wanted a daughter, a choice set in stone, years prior to seeking my assistance in adopting.

An adoption opportunity didn't arise for them right away. When a match was finally made, it came with surprises for me and one for the couple. These surprises involved names.

The couple had chosen the child's middle name long before. Their future daughter would be given a holiday name, a foreign word relating to Christmas. This name also meant "good news" and came from a Latin word meaning birthday. This long-desired bundle of joy was born in December, Christmastime. Her arrival brought very good news for these ecstatic parents.

And then there was the child's chosen first name. When I learned what the name would be, I was amazed. The first name the couple had chosen for their child and the first name of the birth mother were identical. While people often share a first name, this name didn't top any poll of common or trendy names for girls. In fact, it had an old-fashioned vibe.

What are the odds that a name selection made years prior by the adoptive couple would match the circumstances of their adoptive placement? Certainly, it's a longshot at best. Nevertheless, this little girl's parents, as well as I, saw it as God's advance plan to answer the couple's prayers to add a baby girl to their family in His time.

Faith Lesson

> *You will conceive and give birth to a son, and you are to call him Jesus.*
>
> —Luke 1:31

God has plans for us, and He knows what our future holds. His vision isn't general. He knows the very details of what's in store. Let's take Mary for instance. God knew not only that she would bear a child but also that it would be a boy and that His name would be Jesus.

Unfortunately, for the rest of us, God doesn't always reveal what's ahead. We can lift our prayers to Him as to how we would like the future to unfold—perhaps the blessing of a child, the mercy of healing, the provision of a job. He may answer that prayer in the affirmative, but the answer may take some time to be fulfilled.

Hindsight being 20/20, we can often look back and see that God was in control and had a plan for us all along. What was revealed to Mary came to pass just as was revealed to her by the angel. The adoptive parents in this adoption story can certainly be placed in this category. Years before they had prayed for a baby girl. While the answer they received may not have been in the time frame they desired (the sooner the better!) or in the manner anticipated (a biological child), God did answer it. And the circumstances of the answer, specifically the child's name, leave no doubt that His hand was on it.

Lesson Learned: God knows the plans He has for you.

 Baby Steps to Growing Faith

1. Do you assume God has denied your prayer request when it isn't answered immediately?

2. Identify an instance in your life when, looking back, you can see that God had a long-term plan for you all along.

3. How does it make you feel when you see "God winks" in your life such as the adoptive parents did with the name of their child corresponding to the birth mother's first name and the time of year of their daughter's birth?

4. If God knows the future and loves us, why is it so hard for us to trust Him to answer our prayers in the way that is best for us?

Adventure 13

The Black Sheep

Birth mothers don't get pregnant by themselves. For every woman considering an adoptive placement, there's a man in the story somewhere. Despite women who claim the birth father "isn't in the picture," a man played a starring role at the time of conception, and he must be dealt with in the legal proceedings for an adoption.

Who are these men who become birth fathers? Are they simply young and irresponsible males? Certainly older, wiser, and established men wouldn't find themselves in such a predicament—or would they? Some of the men who end up as birth fathers in adoption cases might shock you.

While families often have a black sheep, so do some church congregations. In one of my cases, the birth father was a church elder. Could the scenario be any worse? Unfortunately, yes. This man was much older than the birth mother—definitely old enough to know better—and married. And the birth mother was the church's young secretary.

Unsurprisingly, the birth father wanted the matter to be kept quiet, although it is unclear how he expected God not to know about the sin committed and the resulting pregnancy. One way to keep things mum, at least from fellow church members, was to hide the evidence. In this case, a bulging belly was a dead giveaway, so the birth father urged the birth mother to step away from her position at the church. To avoid gossip, condemnation, and perhaps having to lie about who her baby's father was, the birth mother willingly left her job and pursued an adoptive placement of her child.

Of course, God uses all circumstances for good. Out of this mess came an answer to prayer for a Christian couple desiring a baby to expand their family. While their hearts were full, my heart was broken over the circumstances providing them with a baby.

Faith Lesson

> *All we like sheep have gone astray; we have turned every one to his own way; and the LORD hath laid on him the iniquity of us all.*
>
> —Isaiah 53:6 KJV

When the Bible says "all" of us have gone astray like sheep, it uses the word literally. *All* means all. Every human being has sinned. And getting saved doesn't keep us from sinning because we remain human. Yes, regular churchgoers and church officials sin, too, because they are human. Believers have the means to avoid judgment for their sins because Jesus paid the price to redeem them.

While it is easy to condemn the "black sheep" church elder who should have known better, who are we to judge him? All of us are baa-d too; we are black sheep/sinners as well. We may not have committed the same sin as the birth father in the story above, but we have sinned nonetheless. Told a little lie? Acted prideful? Treated your neighbor unneighborly? Sin is sin. God is pained by *any* sin committed by His children, and He can't be in the presence of it.

Lesson Learned: All of us have sinned.

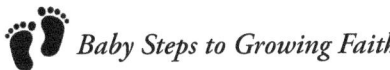 *Baby Steps to Growing Faith*

1. When you mess up, do you see it as a "sin"?

2. Read Isaiah 59:2. Does viewing sin as something separating us from God put it in a different light for you?

3. Does classifying someone else's sin as worse than yours make your sin any less detestable to God?

4. Identify a sin you have committed in the last week. Confess that sin to God and ask His forgiveness.

Adventure 14

Pizza Hut Delivery

According to the familiar kids' song, "First comes love, then comes marriage, then comes a baby in the baby carriage." But babies don't always arrive in a carriage or even by stork. In one adoption case, I delivered a new family member by car—and to a very unlikely destination.

Years ago, hospital policies were not as adoption friendly as they are today. One facility I worked with regularly absolutely refused to allow prospective adoptive parents to come to the hospital, much less the nursery, for the baby's discharge. This stance meant I had to not only go to the hospital with the required legal paperwork to arrange for the baby's discharge but also take an infant carrier and baby clothes to the nursery too. Why? Because I would receive the baby on discharge and transport the bundle of joy to the new parents off the premises.

Where I delivered a baby for placement varied from case to case. The locations ranged from a couple's home to a church and from my office to a local Burger King. But the most memorable delivery made to waiting prospective adoptive parents occurred in the parking lot of a Pizza Hut right near the hospital.

Why, of all places, would someone choose a pizza restaurant for such a momentous occasion? A real estate agent could easily answer this question—location, location, location. That restaurant was the closest place the adoptive couple could get to the hospital to receive physical custody of the baby. The only buildings closer were medical offices with whom I had no connection. How could I say no to such eager and enthusiastic new parents? Pizza Hut it was.

Timing, as they say, is everything. And the time I arrived at Pizza Hut made the occasion even more unforgettable. It was lunchtime, and the restaurant was packed with hungry customers. Little did they know that they were going to be treated to a show in addition to their meal.

As I drove into the packed parking lot, I spotted my clients standing beside their car waiting for me. Even if I hadn't recognized them, the fact that they were holding an infant carrier would've clued me in as to who they were. Toting the carrier, the two raced across the parking lot to meet me. Getting out of my car, I went around to the passenger side of my car and opened the back door to take out the couple's pink bundle of joy. Tears, hugs, and exclamations of delight followed.

Meanwhile, back in the restaurant, diners seated near the windows gawked at the goings-on in the parking lot. Seeing the interest my interaction had garnered, I hoped no one would call the police to report a baby being sold outside Pizza

Personal delivery of a baby girl to her forever family in the Pizza Hut parking lot.

Hut. Fortunately, no cruisers appeared, and the happy couple took their special Pizza Hut delivery with them and went home. They received an answer to prayer to expand their family, and I experienced a unique baby placement that makes for a great story and a big smile on the face of anyone hearing it.

Faith Lesson

> *"But you, Bethlehem Ephrathah,*
> *though you are small among the clans of Judah,*
> *out of you will come for me*
> *one who will be ruler over Israel,*
> *whose origins are from of old,*
> *from ancient times."*

—Micah 5:2

God's ways simply are not our ways. Who would have expected Him to select the tiny village of Bethlehem to produce the Messiah? Why would the people's anticipated king be born in the hill country? Wouldn't the big city of Jerusalem be a more likely and fitting location for a future ruler? But Jesus's birth in a humble place makes His story even more wondrous.

Believers won't forget Bethlehem as the Messiah's delivery location any more than I could forget my Pizza Hut delivery. My clients desired to expand their family through adoption, but I'm positive receiving their new family member in a Pizza Hut parking lot wasn't even on their radar. Leave it to God to provide blessings with an unusual twist.

Lesson Learned: God's ways are not our ways.

Baby Steps to Growing Faith

1. Think of a time when God answered a prayer of yours in an unusual way.

2. When you ask God for something, do you also have in mind just how you want Him to provide it to you?

3. If you receive something you want in an unusual or unexpected way, does it make you wonder if God might be behind it?

4. The next time you make a prayer request, ask God for what you want but then expressly tell Him you trust Him and will accept Him providing the answer in the way He knows is best for you.

Adventure 15

For Such a Time as This

Informing a prospective adoptive couple a match has fallen through is one of the toughest tasks for an adoption professional. There's no easy way to blow up someone's world. Relaying this bad news is like stabbing someone in the heart and then twisting the knife. Saying "I'm sorry" seems lame and vastly inadequate.

Because these events are traumatic for both the person delivering the news and the couple receiving the news, they are seared into one's brain.

As awful as the experience was, I fondly remember one such exchange with a prospective couple who had great insight into what had happened.

This husband and wife really wanted to adopt a baby, but they did not lose sight of the fact that this opportunity came to them as the result of difficult circumstances for the birth mother. The young woman with whom they were matched struggled both emotionally and financially, and the prospective adoptive parents wanted to assist her as best they could within the bounds of the law.

As permitted by Florida adoption law, financial assistance was provided to help the birth mother with some of her necessary living expenses. But the couple didn't just throw money at the woman.

They cared about her as a person and regularly prayed for her. Each time I called them with an update from a doctor's appointment or other news about the birth mother, they made sure to ask me to let the birth mother know they were praying for her.

Then came the day when the birth mother decided to parent her child. While that was her choice and her legal right to do so, the task fell to me to advise my clients the placement would not go forward. The husband and wife were such sweet and caring people. It didn't seem fair that they couldn't have biological children and now their planned adoptive placement had failed.

The wife's response to hearing the bad news amazed me. Although obviously disappointed, she pointed out that perhaps God had not put them in this situation to obtain a baby. Maybe the focus was supposed to be on the birth mother. This couple may have been matched with her so she would have someone to be there for her—someone to love, care for, support, and pray for her—something she lacked in her life. I was floored by these words.

Subsequently this couple received the placement of a baby. The fall-through match preceding it, though, highlighted the for-such-a-time-as-this way God sometimes works.

Faith Lesson

> *And who knows but that you have come to your royal position for such a time as this?*
>
> —Esther 4:14

The opening line of Rick Warren's book *The Purpose Driven Life* states: "It's not about you." It's human nature to assume whatever circumstances we are in are all about us. But sometimes God places us in a position for someone else's benefit. In the Bible, Esther came to be the queen. But her high position wasn't about her. Instead, her position in the court allowed her to take steps to save her people, the Jews. Had she not been there to intercede, they—and possibly she as well—would've been slaughtered by command of the king.

The same can be said about another royal—the King of Kings. Jesus's appearance on earth wasn't about Him. His position as an earthly teacher led Him to serve as a living sacrifice and a means of redemption to those who would accept Him. We can attain eternal life because of the "such a time as this" for which He came.

Lesson Learned: God places us in circumstances to fulfill a role *He* has for us.

 Baby Steps to Growing Faith

1. Have you ever found yourself in certain circumstances thinking you are there for one reason but found that, in fact, God had you there for something entirely different?

2. Does understanding that God places us in certain circumstances for a specific role He wants us to fulfill help you realize He has a plan for us?

3. Does this story underscore that what we often see as being about us may, in fact, be for someone else?

4. Identify a time you found yourself in a position you believe God placed you in. Why do you think God placed you there?

Adventure 16

The Curve

Many of the birth mothers I worked with had no means to come to my office to meet with me. This inability may have stemmed from distance, lack of transportation, or an empty gas tank they couldn't afford to fill. So, I went to them.

These treks were already challenging given the circumstances for the meeting. But merely being able to find the meeting location was daunting in the pre-GPS days. Maps of various cities filled the side pockets of the front doors on my car. While I could ask the woman to provide with me directions to the rendezvous point, that method had its drawbacks.

Case in point? An interesting trip I undertook to Panama City. The meeting point? The motel where the birth mother lived. Just to be clear, neither Holiday Inn, Hilton, nor Best Western appeared on the site's sign. This place would be more aptly described as a "no-tell motel"—a term I first heard in college—offering hourly rates. Duty called, so I couldn't quibble about meeting at a seedy spot; you go where the work is.

I had no clue as to the location of this establishment. The birth mother informed me over the phone that the motel would be easy to find. Before beginning with specific instructions, she asked me,

"Do you know where the curve is on Thomas Drive?" I answered in the affirmative, remembering that the road followed the shoreline and curved at some point. "Well, I live a few doors down from there on the right."

These directions seemed simple enough, and I didn't give the logistics of getting to the destination much thought. Well, at least until I was driving down Thomas Drive with my witness for the paperwork. Passing the place where the road bent to follow the shoreline, we started looking for the no-tell motel. But where was it? I began to be concerned as my car proceeded farther and farther away from the curve in the road.

And then came my "aha!" moment. There on the right side of the road as plain as day was "The Curve." It wasn't a curve in the road but a strip joint and the birth mother's place of employment. Her "home," the no-tell motel, was conveniently located a short distance away for ease of walking to work.

Of course, fits of laughter followed, but upon regaining my composure, I shook my head. Why in the world would the birth mother think that I, a female attorney from a town over an hour away, would have any personal knowledge of the location of a strip club there? I guess her job site was well known among the circles in which she ran. But despite the directions hiccup, I thanked God the birth mother desired to meet with me at her "home" rather than her "office."

Faith Lesson

> *When the teachers of the law who were Pharisees saw him eating with the sinners and tax collectors, they asked his*

disciples: "Why does he eat with tax collectors and sinners?"
—Mark 2:16

Had anyone spotted me entering the no-tell motel for my business meeting, I might have received flak for my choice of companions. How could a respectable *Christian* attorney hang out in a questionable establishment with a *stripper*? My answer would have to be, "WWJD?" Yes, He'd have been right there with me.

The Pharisees and teachers of the law asked the same thing about Jesus. He ate with (gasp!) sinners and tax collectors. That's exactly where God wanted Jesus to be—showing love to those unloved by society and offering them a road to redemption.

Humans tend to be superficial. It's not where we are that matters most; it's *why* we are there. Look beyond the person or the place and identify the purpose. Jesus expressly told believers what our purpose is in life. We are to go into all the world and tell others the good news (Mark 16:15). And isn't a seedy motel just down from a strip club part of "all the world"?

Lesson Learned: It's not where we are but why we are there.

 *Baby Steps to Growing Faith*

1. When Jesus said "all the world," did He literally mean *all* the world?

2. Have you ever judged someone simply because of the place where you saw them or heard they were? Did you stop to consider why they were there?

3. Is a person's need to hear the good news diminished by where they hang out or what they do for a living?

4. Do you resist interacting with those considered disreputable because of what others might think of you?

Adventure 17

"I Can't Bear It!"

Health studies indicate psychiatric disorders are common in women in their childbearing years.[4] Although I have no medical background, my personal experience in years of working with pregnant women considering adoption confirms this conclusion. Mental health issues may be treated with psychiatric medications, but traditionally these medications are discontinued during pregnancy out of fear of the effects on the fetus. This position is good for the baby's protection, but it can make life a living hell for birth mothers who go off their psych meds.

What happens when a woman whose mental health has been stabilized by medication quits taking it? Have you ever heard of Dr. Jekyll and Mr. Hyde? That's your answer. In *The Strange Case of Dr. Jekyll and Mr. Hyde*, Robert Louis Stevenson created a main character with an alter ego exhibiting wildly contradictory behavior. I witnessed such a situation with a birth mother in the early years of my practice. Off her meds, she would morph from Dr. Jekyll into Ms. Hyde in the blink of an eye.

---

4   Randy K. Ward and Mark A. Zamorski, "Benefits and Risks of Psychiatric Medications During Pregnancy," *American Academy of Family Physicians* 66, no. 4 (2002): 629–37, https://www.aafp.org/pubs/afp/issues/2002/0815/p629.html.

Fortunately, this pregnant woman lived approximately an hour from my office. Her location spared us from her simply dropping in to see us. But, unlike most birth mothers, she called us regularly—too regularly for our taste. Don't get me wrong. She was a sweet girl who recognized she simply was in no position to raise a baby. She had more than she could handle dealing with her own demons. I admired her for coming to that conclusion and taking a tough path to provide a good life for her baby.

Nevertheless, no matter how sweet she could be, she had a dark side that reared its ugly head in a snap with no warning. One moment we'd be discussing the date of her next OB appointment, and the next I'd have to hold the phone away from my ear to protect my eardrum from her screaming and my sensibilities from her profane language. These tirades could last for minutes (seemingly hours to whomever was listening to her) and were quite draining and upsetting.

Hanging up wasn't an option. The mentally tortured girl needed our help. She was going through enough already, and we didn't want to upset her even further. The thought of how much her unborn child needed a stable home gave us strength to endure what we heard on the phone line when she became Ms. Hyde.

Being required to listen to such outbursts emotionally drained our staff. To protect our own sanity, we informally agreed to take turns fielding calls from her. When the receptionist announced that this birth mother was on the line, the immediate response tended to be, "It's not my turn! I talked to her last. You take it!" Whoever drew the short straw had to suck it up and take one for the team. Putting the receiver down and concentrating on something else became a coping mechanism. If you could still hear her voice, her rampage continued. When quiet finally occurred, you'd better pick up the phone. She couldn't bear her mental state, and we had a hard time bearing its manifestation.

After the baby's birth and placement, the birth mother resumed her psychiatric medication regimen. And it worked. She became a nice, pleasant, and easy-to-talk-to woman. She appreciated our help and repeatedly thanked us for it. Emails expressing her gratitude were sent to us for some time, and yearly she'd remember us with Christmas cards. Eventually we lost touch, but I'd like to believe that between her prescribed mental health medications and our assistance with her child's placement in a loving home, she is now able to bear her life.

Faith Lesson

> *Be patient, bearing with one another in love.*
> —Ephesians 4:2

As Dad used to say when I'd complain, "No one ever said life was going to be easy." The Christian life isn't always easy either. Why do I say this? That's what the Bible says. We are directed to bear with one another in love.

The verb *bear* does not have a positive connotation. The *Cambridge Dictionary* defines the word as meaning to endure.[5] We endure things like financial difficulties, an illness, or a disappointment. These are not pleasant situations. Basically, we must put one foot in front of the other and just get through it.

---

5 Cambridge Dictionary, "bear," accessed August 15, 2024, https://dictionary.cambridge.org/dictionary/english/bear.

Dealing with others is often a test of your endurance. There are some people we don't like or sometimes just can't stand, to be honest. But our feelings do not matter. God wants us to be patient with those people. Why? They are His children too. He loves them and is patient with them. He expects the same from us.

While bearing with others isn't easy, it might be easier with a different attitude. Focus on *why* you are conducting yourself that way. That individual is a child of the God who loves you so much He sent His Son to sacrifice Himself to save us from our sins. If He can exhibit love to that extent, can't we show our love for Him by exhibiting love to others by being patient with them? Easier said than done, but sometimes God requires us to grin and bear it.

Lesson Learned: We are called by Jesus to bear with others for the greater good.

Baby Steps to Growing Faith

1. If being able to play a musical instrument takes practice, why wouldn't being patient also take practice, such as learning to deal with trying circumstances?

2. Does bearing something mean you have to like or enjoy it? Think of someone who is difficult to be around or whom you don't like. How patient are you with that person?

3. What could you do to be more patient?

4. Identify a time when God may have had to bear with you. Does His ability to endure disobedience or our lack of attention to Him demonstrate His patience?

Adventure 18

Seeing Evil

Evil is an abstract concept. Its presence, however, can be both felt and seen. If I didn't believe that before, I certainly did after an unsettling visit to a birth father in jail.

This man in his mid to late twenties had a criminal history as long as my arm. If his first offense could be characterized as a "mistake" or a "lapse in judgment," he clearly didn't learn from it. He was a multiple repeat offender.

One of his offenses served as the reason I entered the picture. Old enough to know better, the now incarcerated man thought it would be great fun to get involved with a much younger girl—one about half his age. When I say "involved," I mean he engaged in sexual relations with a minor and impregnated her. While not caught in the act per se, the girl's parents did find the birth father hiding in their daughter's closet late one night.

Given the circumstances of the conception and the birth mother's young age, she and her family decided to pursue an adoption. But this legal process required the birth father to be identified and dealt with. So I had to go to the local jail and meet with him.

While not a particularly pleasant place (and it shouldn't be, given its purpose), the jail concerned me far less than its resident

I had to meet. Having to be in the presence of a man with an extensive criminal history made me uneasy.

Cleared to enter the facility, a correctional officer escorted me back to where the public is not allowed. I took a seat in a very small room set aside for attorneys to meet with inmates privately.

Evil was embodied in a prisoner I met at this jail.

The surroundings were stark—four bare walls, a utilitarian metal table, and two chairs. For my safety, the sturdy door to the room held a small window at face level for guards to check on my well-being.

A few minutes later, a man in an orange jumpsuit (required prisoner garb) entered and took the chair across from me. The temperature in the tiny room seemed to have dropped a few degrees. I felt a chill. Then I looked into the birth father's eyes. All I can say is that pure, unadulterated evil looked back at me. While I don't remember our conversation, the look in his eyes remains seared into my memory.

Was the man repentant? Cooperative? Concerned about what was best for his child? No, no, and no. He vowed to fight the adoption. He wanted "his" child. More likely he wanted to cause trouble for the birth mother's parents who'd called the police on him.

He continued his resistance for a few years. Perhaps it gave him something to pass the time to be a jailhouse lawyer and prepare paperwork to oppose the adoption. Finally, and I mean, *finally*, when his child was kindergarten age, we were at last able to achieve termination of his parental rights. We could finalize an adoption for the loving Christian couple she'd been with since birth. Best of all, the child would never have to personally see the look of evil in her biological father's eyes.

Faith Lesson

> *Surely he recognizes deceivers;*
> *and when he sees evil, does he not take note?*
> —Job 11:11

Everyone's heard how to handle evil. We aren't supposed to see it, hear it, or speak it. That's a tall order for us. And to make things more difficult, we are surrounded by others who are also tempted to engage in sin and may entice us to play with the fire of evil.

To protect ourselves from evil, we must recognize what it is. While some evil is readily apparent, other times it is insidious and lurking. Seeing it in others around us may be particularly difficult. How can we know what someone is thinking or feeling? We need help to do that.

Who better to turn to for that assistance than God? He knows each one of His children intimately. In fact, He's known all about us since we were in our mothers' wombs. God, who cannot be in the presence of sin (evil) is able to sense it and identify it. A close relationship with Him is imperative. He can provide us with the ability to discern evil in our daily lives.

Lesson Learned: Evil is real and can be discerned by believers.

Baby Steps to Growing Faith

1. How do you recognize evil?

2. Is evil always readily apparent?

3. What is the hardest for you not to do—speak evil, hear evil, or see evil?

4. Identify a situation in your life where you may need God to provide discernment about evil. Pray and ask Him to help you.

Adventure 19

"Boss of the Babies"

Noises filled the air at the child development center: "Bang, bang, bang" from toddlers bashing toys against any surface they could find; "Waaah!" from more than one infant seeking adult attention; "Stop that!" on a seeming loop from the mouths of teachers on the scene. But in one room of the facility, noise wasn't what was filling the air.

The grins on the children's faces in this classroom and the students hurrying to obey their teacher's directive to sit cross-legged in a circle on the floor belied their excitement. Today was a special day for these pint-sized pupils, a day for sharing. The activity wasn't show-and-tell. Nothing would be shown. Only telling would take place. Each student in turn would be given the chance to explain to their classmates what their mother or father did for a job. The wriggling children finally settled down, and their explanations began.

The teacher listened in amusement as childlike descriptions of various occupations were offered by the young speakers. Because of the center's location in a military community, several students mentioned their parents wore uniforms to work. One girl's mother helped sick people working as a nurse. All were familiar jobs to these little ears.

Then came Kevin's turn. The fair-skinned boy spoke confidently about the important job his mother did. Proudly he stated, "My mom's the boss of the babies. She tells the babies where to go." His classmates didn't understand, but the teacher smiled knowingly. Kevin's mother (me!) worked as an adoption attorney handling the placement of infants from the hospital. Yes, in the end she placed a baby in a specific home, thereby basically telling the baby where to go.

How did Kevin know what my job entailed? Sometimes my family accompanied me to the hospital when I had a weekend placement to handle. We'd make the best of the situation and turn it into a family outing, perhaps going out to eat or grabbing ice cream on the way home. While I went upstairs to arrange for a baby's discharge, Kevin stayed downstairs in the lobby with his sister and my husband. He then observed me coming downstairs with a nurse holding the baby and a happy-looking couple alongside us. I'd direct the nurse to give the baby to the adoptive parents as we reached the exit. In his young mind, I was telling the baby where to go.

As Kevin grew older, so did his understanding of the adoption process. After he turned eighteen, he even accompanied

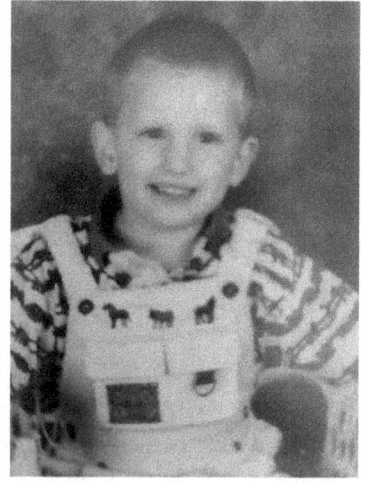

Preschool picture of the Boss of the Babies' baby boy.

me to the hospital occasionally to serve as a witness when a birth mother signed a consent to adoption. He's asked insightful questions about the legal procedure to help him understand it better. Nevertheless, despite becoming an adult and acquiring knowledge about adoption, he still refers to me as the Boss of the Babies. And, come to think of it, the description fits.

Faith Lesson

> *When Jesus came to the region of Caesarea Philippi, he asked his disciples, "Who do people say the Son of Man is?"*
> *They replied, "Some say John the Baptist; others say Elijah; and still others, Jeremiah or one of the prophets."*
> *"But what about you?" he asked. "Who do you say I am?"*
> *Simon Peter answered, "You are the Messiah, the Son of the living God."*
>
> —Matthew 16:13–16

Just as children come to know who their parents are, believers also learn who their heavenly Father is. The realization of His identity is crucial not only to our attaining eternal life but to growing a closer relationship with Him.

Our journey of discovery about God, however, must be a personal one. Jesus emphasized that requirement to His disciples. He started out asking what others were saying about Him. The answer was easy because it merely required the disciples to repeat the answers they'd heard. But Jesus didn't stop there. He then queried,

"But what about you?" Jesus needed to know what *their* answers would be. What did they personally believe?

Simon Peter quickly responded, "You are the Messiah, the Son of the living God." How could the disciple reach that conclusion? Because he had spent time in Jesus's presence, traveling with Him, talking with Him, and observing His actions. Simon Peter could see and determine for himself just who Jesus was.

At some point we all must address who we think Jesus is. The answer is much easier to give when we have direct knowledge from our interactions with Him. Just as my son could definitively say who I was from observing what I did firsthand, we can know who Jesus is from spending time with Him and observing the difference He makes not only in our lives but also in those around us.

Lesson Learned: It's important for us to know who Jesus is.

 Baby Steps to Growing Faith

1. Who do you say Jesus is? Why?

2. Why is it important to have a clear understanding of who Jesus is?

3. Who does Jesus say you are to Him?

4. Has your understanding of who Jesus is changed over time? If so, how and why?

Adventure 20

"I Forgot"

It takes two to tango, and it takes two to conceive a baby. Given this latter fact of life, Florida adoption attorneys must always ask who the father is when a birth mother requests assistance in placing her child for adoption. Not a difficult question, right? Apparently, it's more difficult for some than for others. Take this case, for example.

The pregnant woman with whom we were working was quite familiar to us. Why? She would be labeled a "repeat birth mother." This label means she had previously placed a child—actually in her case *children*—through our office. While a sweet girl, she kept making the same mistake over and over.

The mother readily answered our questions about her health and the paternity of the child. She identified a man by name as her baby's biological father, allowing us to take the required steps to address him in the adoption process. The birth father she named cooperated and signed the paperwork we needed to move forward. Smooth sailing, right?

Unfortunately, things hit a big snag after the baby's birth and placement with the prospective adoptive parents. In keeping with standard procedure, I requested a copy of the baby's original birth certificate from Florida's Office of Vital Statistics. Imagine my surprise when this document arrived in the mail bearing the name of a different man as the baby's father. What?

Under Florida law, no man can be placed on the birth certificate unless he is the birth mother's husband (and thus the child's legal father) or he signed the application for the birth certificate acknowledging he was the father. Bottom line? The unmarried birth mother knew who this man was, and he showed up at the hospital to sign the birth certificate application.

This turn of events threw a monkey wrench into our case. We now had a legal father (a man identified as the father on a legal document) to address in the court proceedings. A call to the birth mother for an explanation was in order.

What did she have to say about this important omission from the facts about her child's paternity. "I forgot about him." Say what? How do you forget about a possible father of the child you are carrying? You forget to buy milk at the store, or you forget it's someone's birthday, not a recent sexual partner who may have impregnated you. And, if indeed the birth mother had brain fog from her pregnancy, why didn't she immediately inform us when she "remembered" at the hospital to allow him to sign the birth certificate application?

The birth mother's memory was obviously questionable. She forgot something huge. Me? I'll never forget this incident of her forgetting.

Faith Lesson

> *"But they, our ancestors, became arrogant and stiff-necked, and they did not obey your commands. They refused to*

> *listen and failed to remember the miracles you performed among them."*
>
> —Nehemiah 9:16–17

Failing to remember some things is understandable. Who hasn't had to search for car keys or a cell phone because they couldn't remember where they placed the missing item? But forgetting big things is entirely different.

If you experienced a traumatic event, would you fail to remember it? If you witnessed a miracle, would you forget it? The Israelites, unfortunately, would have to answer both questions in the affirmative. Their people spent years in slavery to the oppressive Egyptians. Then God made a way for them to escape, including the miraculous parting of the Red Sea. But their subsequent actions established that they'd forgotten what God had done. They refused to listen to Him, failed to obey Him, and often whined about the circumstances in which they found themselves.

Why did the Israelites fail to remember God's care for them in the recent past? Because they were too busy focusing on themselves and their current situation. This behavior robbed them of peace of mind and a close relationship with God. Had they remembered what He had previously done for them, they would be filled with gratitude for His love and care, assured He had their best interest in mind, and engaged in a good (not strained) relationship with Him.

When complaining and chafing at obeying God's commands, just stop for a moment. Think of what we should remember about our heavenly Father. Let's focus on who He is and what He's done for us rather than on our circumstances and what we want.

Lesson Learned: We tend to forget the things God has done for us.

Baby Steps to Growing Faith

1. What's the best way for you to remember something?

2. How would you feel if someone forgot something big you had done for them?

3. Make a list of five wonderful things God has done for you.

4. Take time each morning for the next week to read aloud the list you just made.

Adventure 21

Peer Pressure

Along with the terrible twos, a child's teenage years test their parents' sanity. Teenagers live in the moment, are hormone-driven, and know everything despite lack of life experience.

But one teenage birth mother amazed me. A high school student, she unexpectedly found herself pregnant. With good grades, her future seemed bright—until the pregnancy, anyway. Her dreams included getting a college education. Being a single mother supporting and raising a child would leave little time and no money for pursuing a college degree.

The decision to place her baby for adoption wasn't merely about her future, though. She had a child to consider. The girl wrestled with several questions as she tried to decide what to do. Didn't her child deserve the best? Wasn't life in a loving and financially stable two-parent home what the innocent child should have? The answer, she maturely determined, was a resounding yes. A well-reasoned decision, though, didn't hurt any less. An adoptive placement meant separation from her child. Her heart ached at that thought.

But the cost of her making an adoptive placement climbed higher than I initially realized. After the baby's birth and placement with an adoptive family, the birth mother revealed another price she paid for choosing the adoption option. The loss of her friends. And, for teenagers, their friends make up their world.

The birth mother hung out with a small group of friends who had known one another for years. When she confided she'd be placing her baby for adoption, they were less than supportive. As it turns out, all of them were teen moms. These girls pointed out to their pregnant friend what fun it would be to raise their kids together, dress them up, and have playdates.

This reaction blew the birth mother's mind. They wanted her to base her decision on what would be fun for *them*? What about her child? Had they even considered how they would be able to raise their own children, given their age and financial situations? All were teenagers living at home and receiving help from their parents, after all.

These friends pressured the birth mother not to make an adoptive placement. When she resisted, they cut her loose. Now she was friendless, pregnant, and facing a future without her child.

"You know," the birth mother confided, "the last few months of my pregnancy were the loneliest time of my entire life. But I had to do what I thought was best for my child."

"You may not raise your child," I told her, "but you acted like a mother with your decision. When you realized you couldn't provide for your child, you made sure your little one would be in a place where her needs would be met. Your choice made it possible for her to be raised in a loving, two-parent home."

Words cannot express how much I admired that teenager. She'd made a mature decision based on her love for her child. In doing so, she resisted the forceful pressure of her peers. And not just any peers but her circle of friends, now her ex-friends.

Faith Lesson

> *Do not follow the crowd in doing wrong.*
> —Exodus 23:2

What's the worst thing that can happen if you fail to go along with the crowd? A decline in your social standing? Loss of "friends" on social media? In the case of a man named Daniel, his very life depended on going along with the crowd.

Daniel lived as a Jew in exile in Babylon. While he may not have resided in his home country, he did quite well for himself with a secure government position. But some of the "in" crowd didn't like him. They suggested to King Darius that he enter a decree requiring everyone to worship and pray only to him. Anyone worshipping another god would meet a rather nasty end: they'd be tossed into the lion's den for lion chow.

Undaunted by what everyone else was doing, Daniel continued to worship the one true God. He even prayed to Him from his upstairs room with the windows open so anyone could see what he was doing. Daniel's intentional decision not to follow the crowd enraged his fellow government workers who tattled on him to the king.

A trip to the lion's den for Daniel ensued. But God looked out for Daniel. The lions left him alone, and God's power was displayed to a heathen king. Not following the crowd was the best choice Daniel could have made.

In my adoption adventure, the teenage birth mother's choice not to cave and do what her friends were doing figuratively saved her child's life. Instead of being raised by a struggling, very young single mother, the little one received a stable home with two loving parents. The birth mother could now pursue a college education with the knowledge she'd done right by her child. Her decision not to follow the crowd, although bringing her sadness, certainly spoke to her friends about priorities and earned her my respect and admiration.

Lesson Learned: Don't just go along with others; do the right thing.

 Baby Steps to Growing Faith

1. What's something you've been tempted to do because "everyone else," or at least some people you know, were doing it?

2. Is the fact others are doing something reason enough to do it too?

3. Did Jesus do what those in a position of power, such as the Pharisees, did? If He didn't follow the crowd in doing wrong, do you think He wants you to?

4. Are you focused on what the crowd is doing or what Jesus would have you do? Identify a step you can take to focus on Him more and then take it.

Adventure 22

All I Want for Christmas

Preschoolers darted about the playground, excitedly discussing what they wanted for Christmas. With the holiday approaching later that month, gifts would be received in just a matter of days. Eyes were shining and bright in anticipation.

Watching over the outdoor activity of her young charges, a young woman stood nearby. Hearing what the children desired for Christmas brought a smile to the teacher's lips, but the ache remained in her heart. She would not get what she wanted for Christmas—a baby for her and her husband to love.

A little girl skipped up to her teacher with a big smile on her face. "What do you want for Christmas, Mrs. Smith?" she asked.

With a catch in her voice, the teacher responded, "My husband and I would really like to have a baby, but I don't think we can get one for Christmas."

Without skipping a beat, the child said, "Well, if you want a baby, you need to ask God for one." Then she dropped to her knees, clasped her small hands together, closed her eyes, and prayed out loud. "God, please give Mrs. Smith a baby for Christmas. She really wants one." Rising, she ran off to join her classmates.

Later that month, I was looking forward to some time at home with my family for Christmas. But babies don't respect holidays and continue to be born on or near them. A couple of days before Christmas, our office received a call from a hospital in Pensacola about a drop-in birth mother, one who simply showed up and gave birth with no prior medical care. She wanted to place her newborn for adoption but had no plans in place. Could we help? Of course we could!

But helping came at a personal cost. It required me to drive to the hospital just a little over an hour away on Christmas Eve to take the birth mother's consent and arrange for the baby's discharge to the prospective adoptive couple. *What else did I have to do?* I thought sarcastically. But my irritation turned to guilt for thinking that thought when I watched the husband and wife greet their new family member in the hospital. After all, wasn't Christmas Eve really all about the joy of a baby's arrival?

Following the baby's holiday placement with the couple, I moved forward with the court proceedings to finalize the adoption. During those weeks, I was in regular contact with the new parents. In one phone conversation, the wife remarked that, in all the excitement of the last-minute placement, she'd neglected to tell me part of the back story.

My client related the touching moment her student prayed for God to give her teacher a baby for Christmas. Tears came to my eyes as I heard what God had done for this couple. But I was also amazed at the faith of a little child that paved the way for an adoptive placement. She asked, and God had answered. The child believed God could do it, and He did.

Faith Lesson

> *If you believe, you will receive whatever you ask for in prayer.*
> —Matthew 21:22

When Christians ask God for something, they may feel their role in the matter is done. They ask, God answers. Simple as that. But that's not what Jesus said as He walked along the road with His disciples.

Jesus focused on the essential factor of belief after a fig tree failed to offer fruit for His hungry group. Dissatisfied with the tree's production, or rather lack of production, He asked that the fig tree never bear fruit again. Instantly the tree withered, amazing the disciples who witnessed its transformation. They wanted Jesus to explain how that could happen.

Matthew 21:22 offers Jesus's answer. The first three words of the verse, "If you believe," are key. Merely asking God for something isn't sufficient. Belief must accompany the request. The formula Jesus provided is simple to state: ask + believe = answered prayer. But putting that formula into practice can be a stumbling block. *Can/will God do what we've asked of Him?* we wonder.

Perhaps help comes from the scenario preceding Jesus's words. He had just miraculously caused a tree to wither right before the disciples' eyes. They witnessed what God could do. We've all seen what God can do in one way or another. We see the beautiful world He created out of a dark void. We observe how He has answered prayers for those we know. We have even looked on as He answered prayers for us in the past. Remember, seeing is believing. What

He's done previously for us and others allows us to believe and then receive when we ask in His will.

The adoptive couple in this story asked God for something difficult for them to obtain—a baby to adopt privately. But they contacted our office and moved forward in belief even when the answer wasn't immediate like the withering of a fig tree at Jesus's request. They asked, they believed, and they received in God's timing and in accordance with His will.

Lesson Learned: Ask with faith, and in line with God's will, and you will receive.

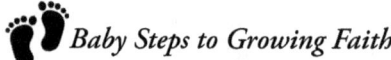
Baby Steps to Growing Faith

1. How are believing and receiving connected?

2. How often do you believe God will answer the prayer you are praying? Or is your request like throwing spaghetti against the wall and hoping it will stick?

3. Why do we think God can't do something we ask of Him if He created the world and raised Jesus from the grave?

4. What things help you to believe? Would keeping a journal of answered prayers bolster your belief? Write down what you ask God for this week and then see how He answers.

Adventure 23

Dressed for Success?

Birth mothers often hide their pregnancy from family, friends, and even the birth father. That may work when her grandmother lives in another state, she only sees certain friends occasionally, and she's no longer dating the birth father. But the secret is harder to keep from someone the birth mother lives with and sees daily. One case we handled took the cake for the birth mother keeping impending motherhood hidden.

"Sherry" contacted our office about placing her unborn child for adoption. The pregnancy was unplanned—very unplanned. Although married, she declared her husband was not the baby's biological father. Therefore, Sherry kept her spouse in the dark about being with child.

As Sherry explained to me, she'd traveled out of state to visit relatives. While there, she attended a party where she met the biological father. The two immediately clicked, and one thing led to another. Shortly thereafter, Sherry learned she was pregnant.

"But since you're married, couldn't your husband be the baby's biological father? You are living with your husband, right?" I asked.

"Yeah, we live together, but we hadn't really been getting along then. So, the guy I met at the party is the only one I had sex with when I could've gotten pregnant. My husband *can't* find out I'm pregnant. He'll know it isn't his."

"How could he know it wasn't his child?"

"The dude from the party was black, and my husband and I are white. My husband would know when he sees the baby. And that would be it for us."

All righty then. No drama in this situation.

Sherry, a thin girl, could have been a model for one of my stick figure drawings. Although she showed a hint of a baby bulge, it could be masked with loose-fitting clothing. For the public, that works, but what about with her husband at home? They slept in the same bed, and certainly he saw her in some state of undress occasionally.

Early one morning, Sherry called the office in a panic. In labor, she needed to go to the hospital, but her husband hadn't left for work yet. Sherry wanted me to come pick her up "right now" and take her to the hospital.

"But what about your husband? What will you tell him?"

"I told him I had a job interview this morning, and that a friend was going to give me a ride."

Racing to my car, I felt almost as panicked as Sherry sounded. *This situation could go south quickly. What if the husband figures out what's going on? What if he asks me how I know Sherry?*

Pulling up to her house a few minutes later, I took a deep breath, raised a prayer for help, and walked quickly to the front door with my heart thumping.

And who should open the door when I rang the doorbell? None other than hubby himself.

"Hi! I'm Alice, and I'm here to take Sherry to her job interview this morning," I announced before he could speak.

Oh, please, Lord! Don't let him ask me where the interview is.

He left the door and called for Sherry. She appeared right away and said, "We'd better go now!"

I gaped at the birth mother's appearance. (Hopefully only inwardly.) Her interview attire consisted of a pair of old sweatpants, sneakers, an oversized T-shirt, and no makeup. She'd look slovenly even interviewing to work at a gym.

Where in the world did she tell her husband she was interviewing? Who'd hire anyone looking like she did? Well, if he's too blind to recognize she's pregnant, I guess he doesn't care what she wears out of the house either.

However, we didn't have the luxury of time to discuss wardrobe selections. I wanted to get back in my car and drive off toward the hospital before the husband reappeared. Fifteen minutes after I dropped Sherry off at the hospital, she gave birth. That was close! She could hide her baby bump from her husband, but I'm not sure she could have hidden a newborn.

Faith Lesson

> *Therefore, as God's chosen people, holy and dearly loved, clothe yourselves with compassion, kindness, humility, gentleness and patience.*
>
> —Colossians 3:12

When Christians go out into the world, we decide how we will clothe ourselves. But that decision has nothing to do with tangible items of clothing nor is it concerned with brands, colors, or trends. Fortunately, a team uniform exists. Paul gave fashion guidance in Colossians 3:12. He didn't mention togas, sandals, or bracelets. However, he stressed that compassion, kindness, humility, gentleness, and patience are the Christian style.

Those internal attributes are reflected in our outer appearance. Others, particularly nonbelievers to whom we are to witness, will take note of how we look. We are patient, kind, gentle, humble, and compassionate, which is at odds with worldly "attire." Our appearance will be so appealing they will want to wear the same thing.

The story of Sherry concerns two clothing situations. She sought to be deceitful with her husband by wearing baggy clothes to conceal her baby bump. Me? I pray that the Christian clothing Sherry saw on me was kindness, compassion, and patience in my efforts to assist her in a difficult time.

Lesson Learned: Christians have a standard uniform in which to clothe themselves.

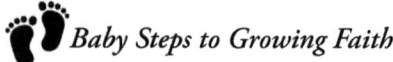
Baby Steps to Growing Faith

1. Why is it that a person's attire is one of the first things you notice about them?
2. Identify two ways in which attributes such as kindness and patience resemble clothing.
3. Which is more important to Jesus, how His followers look or how they treat others?
4. What's a concrete way to clothe yourself with the attributes Paul wrote about in Colossians 3:12?

Adventure 24

Tom, Dick, or Harry?

How do you find out who fathered the child a pregnant woman is carrying? Since birth fathers didn't usually accompany a woman considering an adoptive placement to my office, I had to ask the mother directly about her child's paternity.

I framed the question to a birth mother as delicately as possible. Imagine speaking to someone for the very first time in person and asking them who their sexual partners are or have been. My standard operating procedure was to first apologize for having to ask something of a personal nature. I'd then explain that determining the answer to the question was a legal requirement. But blaming the applicable law doesn't make asking the question any less embarrassing for me. However awkward the asking can be, though, sometimes hearing the answer can make the situation even more awkward.

One of those awkward times for me started off with a pregnant young woman sitting in my office. After the usual pleasantries and my explanation of the adoption process, I got down to brass tacks.

"And who is the baby's father?" I queried, trying to make my voice sound as nonchalant as possible.

"Well, I'm not exactly sure," she responded.

"Can you identify who the possible fathers might be?" I prompted her.

"There are several. It really depends on when the child was conceived. I should find that out when I go for my next doctor's appointment. They'll do an ultrasound then."

We were making progress, but we weren't in the clear yet. I pressed on and noted, "It's important we identify any man who might be a potential father based on the conception time frame. We want to make sure everything is done correctly so no problems pop up down the line."

The birth mother voiced her understanding and promised to call me with the information obtained from her ultrasound results. The baby's measurements would help pinpoint a clear time frame for conception.

The birth mother called me a few weeks later. "I talked to my doctor at my OB appointment and told him it was really important to know when the baby could have been conceived. He narrowed down the conception date to one week. Based on that time frame, there could only be three possible birth fathers."

*Three possible birth fathers? In **one** week? Good thing the doctor didn't give her a month to work with.*

I reiterated the need for our office to contact all three of these men about the intended adoptive placement. They didn't have to agree with her decision, but they did have to be given notice of what she was planning to do.

"But none of them care what I do. Not one of them thinks they're the father."

I assured her contacting these men was a routine step in an adoption. The step had to be taken to pursue a placement. What could she say?

With the identities of the possible birth fathers nailed down, I walked into my boss's office. The "boy attorney," as I teasingly called him, typically handled contact with birth fathers in our adoption cases. We'd found over the years that sometimes a man-to-man conversation works better. A cold call placed to a man to discuss him possibly having impregnated the birth mother we were working with could be awkward, after all.

"Have fun with this one!" I said, smiling and handing him a detailed memo about the three men named by the birth mother.

Of course, it took some time for the "boy attorney" to reach all three possible birth fathers. When I'd check with him about his progress reaching them, we'd refer to the case as the "Tom, Dick, or Harry" one. These weren't their real names, but it was easier to remember. Unsurprisingly to us, each of the men denied paternity when contacted, and the adoption proceeded smoothly to finalization.

Faith Lesson

> *He told her, "Go, call your husband and come back."*
> *"I have no husband," she replied.*
> *Jesus said to her, "You are right when you say you have no husband. The fact is, you have had five husbands, and the man you now have is not your husband. What you have just said is quite true." . . .*

> *"Come, see a man who told me everything I ever did.
> Could this be the Messiah?"*
>
> —John 4:16–18, 29

During a relative's bridal shower, each of the guests received a card listing questions about the bride. I knew some answers off the bat, but some questions stumped me. The purpose of this inquiry? To find out who knew the bride the best. To absolutely no one's surprise, the person answering the most questions correctly, and thus the winner of the party game (drum roll, please), turned out to be her mother.

It makes sense that the person who knows us best when we're in our twenties is likely to be a parent. They've known us from the very beginning and have also known us longer than our college roommates, best friends, and coworkers. But as we grow older, move away from home, or get married, parents aren't necessarily as close as they once were.

Despite changes in our lives, there's someone who knows us better than anyone else regardless of our age. In fact, that someone—God—knows everything about us. He even knows the number of hairs on our head (Luke 12:7). His knowledge is not simply about our physical makeup, such as eye color, or our name, but He is aware of all our thoughts and actions (Psalm 139:2).

The story of the Samaritan woman at the well illustrates the intimate knowledge and understanding God has of our lives. Jesus had never laid physical eyes on her before, yet He was able to recount the trail of broken marriages in this woman's past as well as her current live-in relationship. He knew her best. And, despite her checkered past and present, He still treated her with kindness and gave her His attention. Jesus also allowed this unclean Samaritan woman to hear from His lips that He was the long-awaited Messiah (John 4:26). And He went to the cross to allow everyone, including her, to have a path to salvation.

Like the woman at the well in the Bible story, God knew the birth mother in my adoption adventure better than anyone. Despite His knowledge of her various relationships, He still offers her the way to eternal life. How blessed we are to be loved so much by the one who knows us best—warts and all.

Lesson Learned: Despite knowing all about us, God still loves us.

 *Baby Steps to Growing Faith*

1. Is there anything God doesn't know about you?

2. Would you live your life differently if you truly believed it was an open book to God?

3. How does it make you feel to know God loves you despite His awareness of all your slipups, failures, and disobedience?

4. Identify a lapse you've made in the last week. Talk to God about it. Tell Him you know He already knows about it, but that you want to ask His forgiveness.

Adventure 25

Religiously Following the Rules

The "whew!" moment for me in a baby placement usually came when the birth mother set her pen down after signing a consent to adoption. Why then? A birth mother's choice had been firmly made and evidenced in writing. The next step? Getting the baby discharged from the hospital. That was easy, though, right?

One discharge turned into a figurative battle with a military hospital. No physical ammunition was involved, but a clash of words and wills ensued. The young birth mother recognized and accepted she was in no position to parent her child. Understandably, her emotions churned, so she emphatically told me she didn't want to see the baby after its birth. And she didn't. Well, at least until the baby's discharge.

The attending nurse refused to honor the original post-birth release signed by the birth mother directing the hospital to discharge the baby to me. My attempt to get the hospital to honor that directive was fruitless despite emphasizing that this situation involved an adoption, showing my ID to prove I was the individual named in the release, and even pulling out my Florida Bar card to establish I was a licensed attorney and an officer of the court. The nurse was similarly not swayed by my playing a sympathy card—

the birth mother hadn't seen the baby in the hospital and did not wish to see her child at all because it would be too upsetting to her.

"Are you intentionally going to put your patient through this torture? Is that best for your patient to deal with such trauma in addition to recovering from delivery?" I asked.

Unfortunately, I lost the battle but continued the war by going up the ranks and speaking with the charge nurse. She also shot down my request for the baby to be discharged to me.

My requests were denied because, as the medical staff advised, it was against a military regulation for the baby to be discharged to me. Nevertheless, I persisted in asking questions about this regulation. So the medical staff punted to the JAG (judge advocate general) office, which handles legal affairs.

A nurse directed me to a lounge on the maternity floor to await a lawyer from the JAG office. Either I'd raised a thorny legal issue or the uniform-clad lawyers were bored and wanted to see a legal skirmish because not one, not two, but *three* lawyers showed up. The battle lines were drawn. I sat in a chair holding my pink file with all the paperwork the birth mother had just signed. Directly across from me sat three stern-looking men.

Naively I thought these fellow lawyers would understand the effect of a duly signed, witnessed, and notarized release asking the hospital to discharge the baby to me. I was an attorney, for heaven's sake, not a child stealer. Nope. The signed paper lost the battle when pitted against the unidentified military regulation prohibiting me from taking the baby.

At that point my law school training kicked in. If you can't win based on the law, argue policy. I emphasized that the hospital was a medical center existing to take care of its patient's welfare. Doctors were supposed to do no harm. The young birth mother would suffer unnecessary emotional harm from being forced to see and hold a baby she didn't want contact with and wasn't going to parent.

My compelling (at least to me) argument fell on deaf ears. Unmoved, the legal officers advised me the bottom line was that the birth mother was the only individual who had authority to take the child out of the hospital. Period. The end.

Swallowing the lump in my throat, I headed to the birth mother's room and filled her in on the situation. I apologized profusely for the position the hospital's stance put her in and promised I'd given it my best shot to get the facility to relent. Tearfully, the birth mother agreed to carry the baby downstairs and out to the parking lot.

As soon as the exit's sliding glass doors opened and she stepped outside the hospital, she turned and handed me the baby. I hugged the birth mother, but I couldn't bring myself to look at her as she walked off with her shoulders slumped and tears no doubt pouring from her eyes.

The hospital rules had been observed. But in doing so, the facility put a knife in its patient's heart and twisted it.

Faith Lesson

> *Then he said to them, "The Sabbath was made for man, not man for the Sabbath."*
>
> —Mark 2:27

Parents often lay down the law to their offspring. After being told what to do, the little darlings may come back with that endearing response, "But why?" To which they typically receive the matter-of-fact answer, "Because I said so." With such an upbringing, it's not surprising people fail to consider why a certain rule is in place.

A law-school lesson seems appropriately applied here. Sometimes arguments are most effective when you take a proposition to the extreme. Shall we try it?

The proposition in question? If a rule exists, it must be followed. Let's say your child has stopped breathing and is turning blue. You don't have time to wait for an ambulance to show up, so you put your child in the car and head to the hospital. The speed limit on the road is thirty-five. Do you obey that rule and drive that slowly to the ER with your child's life hanging in the balance? Or do you put the pedal to the metal and exceed the speed limit to get your child the medical help he needs as quickly as possible?

Yes, that situation was extreme, but it points out that sometimes circumstances legitimately exist for not following a rule. A speed limit is in place to protect people's lives. That goal is not achieved if it hampers a motorist from reaching the hospital in an emergency. Likewise, the goal of protecting patients by the regulation put in place at the military hospital was not achieved in the adoption adventure. Rather than protecting a patient, compliance with the rule that only the parent could remove the baby from the hospital wreaked havoc on the birth mother's emotional well-being.

A ban on working on the Sabbath under the Jewish law existed to keep people focused on God by setting aside a day for Him. Jesus was teaching His disciples about God on that Sabbath discussed in Mark 2:27. In fact, God in the person of Jesus walked with those disciples. Sustaining their bodies with needed nourishment by picking heads of grain to eat only facilitated that interaction rather than distracting from it. So Jesus called out those condemning Him for breaking the law by pointing out that religious rules were meant to benefit man, not to hamper him.

Yes, Jesus was a rule breaker. He considered the rule less important than the needs of God's children. Substance is meant to outweigh form.

Lesson Learned: Faith is about substance, not simply rules.

 *Baby Steps to Growing Faith*

1. Does following rules always achieve the reason why they exist?

2. Read Mark 2:23–28. To whom did Jesus say that the Sabbath was made for man and not vice versa? Was Jesus impressed by this group's strict adherence to Jewish law?

3. Is it easier to blindly follow a rule than to consider why the rule was made and if it should be applied under the circumstances? Is blindly following rules the lazy way to proceed?

4. Think of a rule Christians accept such as "Tell the truth." Why does that rule exist? Now, think of a time when it might be permissible not to comply with it [example: to facilitate a surprise party].

Adventure 26

Will the Real Birth Mother Please Stand Up?

Most of the time, the big question in an adoption case is the identity of the baby's father. No question exists about who the mother is, right? She's the one who's visibly pregnant or who's recently given birth to the baby being placed for adoption. But in one strange case, the identity of a newborn's mother became an issue.

Like a bolt from the blue, trouble arrived one day when I reviewed my office mail. Among the envelopes was one from Florida's Office of Vital Statistics (OVS). I regularly received correspondence from OVS with copies of birth certificates I'd requested for adoption proceedings, so nothing was unusual. Yet.

As always, I scanned the baby's birth certificate to make sure the date of birth, child's gender, and name given were correctly recorded. No problems were noted. But then my eye dropped down to the line identifying the birth mother. What? Who was that? The name listed wasn't the name of the visibly pregnant woman with whom I'd worked and who had signed a consent to the adoption at the hospital with me after her baby's birth.

Stunned, I did the only logical thing. I called the woman I knew to be the birth mother for an explanation. Staring at the official birth record in my hand, I asked her, "Who's 'Jane Doe'?" Turns out, Jane was her sister.

Sheepishly, the girl confessed what she had done. Her picture ID was lost, and she hadn't replaced it. When she left for the hospital to give birth, she simply "borrowed" her sister's ID and produced it as her own ID when asked. The two women looked alike, and no one at the hospital raised a concern that the woman in a hospital gown in labor didn't look exactly like the picture on her ID. (But maybe they should have.)

When I met with the birth mother in the hospital after the baby's birth, I had no need to look at the ID she had with her. I recognized her from our prior interactions. A copy of her real picture ID, prior to its loss, was also in my file from our first meeting at my office. So I was clueless that the birth mother was masquerading as her sister with the hospital.

Once the listed birth mother mystery was solved, I then had to figure out how to get the real mother's name on the birth certificate instead. Why? The birth certificate is filed in an adoption case to establish the birth mother's identity. Under Florida law, the required consent of the identified mother must be obtained. Calling OVS, I learned no change to the birth certificate could be made without a court order.

I dutifully filed a motion making a request for that order, supporting it with a sworn statement of the real birth mother. The presiding judge granted my motion, and OVS subsequently issued a corrected birth certificate—one naming the actual birth mother. The judge later told me this situation was a first for him, and I assured him it was for me too. And, thankfully, no second time ever arose.

Faith Lesson

> *No one who practices deceit*
> *will dwell in my house;*
> *no one who speaks falsely*
> *will stand in my presence.*
> —Psalm 101:7

God detests lies and deceit. And pretending to be someone you're not falls squarely into that category. It involves lying about who you are and deceiving someone about your identity.

Why would a person claim to be someone else? It's probably because that deception is an easy way out of dealing with a troubling situation. Being honest would just make things more complicated, they think. But what is perceived as a snap solution merely leads into deeper trouble.

Take a sister story from the Bible, for example. In Genesis 12, Abram and his wife, Sarai, decided to move to Egypt during a severe famine. Before entering Egypt, Abram told his wife to identify herself as his sister. Because of her beauty, Abram was afraid the Egyptian men would desire Sarai and kill him to get to her if they knew they were husband and wife. And his plan worked. Perhaps it worked too well. The Egyptians fell for the story that Sarai was Abram's sister, so Pharaoh decided to take Sarai as his own. He had her brought to his palace and treated Abram, her supposed brother, well.

So things got complicated. The spouses were separated with Sarai at the palace with the pharaoh, who would likely make her yet another of his wives. Deceit had merely caused Sarai and Abram more trouble. Similarly, things got complicated when the birth mother misrepresented herself as her sister at the hospital. Yes, there would've been an issue without an ID for the birth mother to present, but it was an issue that could have been resolved. It was much more complicated, and involved court proceedings, to undo the consequences of her pretense of being her sister.

Life is messy, and God knows it. But He is the truth (John 14:6) and expects His followers to be honest and tell the truth. The easy way out using lies and deceit leads to more complications. Worse yet, it results in separation from God

Lesson Learned: God despises deceit.

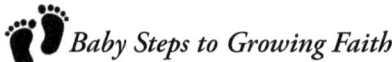
Baby Steps to Growing Faith

1. Think of a time when you were deceitful about something. What motivated you to do so?

2. How do you feel when someone is deceitful with you? Does it negatively affect your relationship with them?

3. Read John 14:6. If Jesus is described as the truth, do you think He wants to be around deceit?

4. Is deceitfulness limited to verbal representations such as Sarai claiming Abram was her brother? How about actions? If a Christian's walk doesn't match his talk, is he being deceitful with himself and others about his relationship with God?

Adventure 27

Miss Kitty

It was her big day. The precious little girl's adoption would be finalized in a hearing at the courthouse. While her family talked excitedly in the hallway outside the judge's office, the three-year-old explored the strange new place they'd brought her. The bundle of energy and curiosity flitted about like a butterfly.

Called into the judge's office for the hearing, the adults quietly filed in and took their seats. The little girl squirmed trying to get down from the lap where she perched. She wanted to check out the new room.

The judge briefly distracted the youngest person at the hearing by commenting on her pretty clothes. Mom had dolled her up for the occasion, and other family members wore a bit dressier attire than usual. The child, however, was more interested in knickknacks in the judge's office than her outfit. The hearing lasted only a few minutes, a good thing since the new adoptee's patience for being held still had worn thin.

As I walked into the hallway outside the judge's office, I explained to the clients what happened next. Yes, the adoption had been legally finalized, but we had to obtain documentation from the clerk to establish that fact. Specifically, a certified copy of the

Final Judgment of Adoption was needed to request a new birth certificate showing the adoptive couple as the child's parents and bearing the child's adopted name.

While her parents listened attentively to my explanation, their daughter fidgeted. She was tired of standing there. Thinking the idea of movement would pacify her, I looked down at her and said in a cheery voice, "We are going to walk down to the end of this hall and see Miss Kitty." The little one's face brightened, and she eagerly held my hand as we proceeded down the hall.

Entering the Clerk of Court's office, I looked around and spotted Kitty, the clerk who usually processed adoption paperwork for me. She smiled and came over to the counter where our group stood. "We have a very special girl with us today," I said, pointing at the adoptee. Looking at the adoptee, I then told her, "This is Miss Kitty."

A frown crossed the adorable girl's face. "But where's the kitty? I want to see the kitty!"

The adults laughed as I explained to the child we had come to meet this nice lady, Miss Kitty, who would help us with some papers her parents needed. "No cats are allowed in the courthouse," I added. Her crestfallen look said it all.

Kitty helpfully provided us with the certified copies requested as quickly as she could. The child perked up

Miss Kitty was a sweet clerk at the courthouse, not a cat.

when her parents received their paperwork and learned they could now leave and go celebrate. *Hopefully at a McDonald's with a playground so she can burn off some energy*, I thought. While the adoptive parents would look back at coming to the courthouse with joy, if the little one remembered it later, she would no doubt focus on the disappointment of not meeting a kitty.

Faith Lesson

> *"For my thoughts are not your thoughts,*
> *neither are your ways my ways,"*
> *declares the LORD.*

—Isaiah 55:8

The Old Testament is replete with references to the promised Messiah. While scholars disagree on exactly how many exist, the possibilities number in the hundreds. From these prophecies, the Jews clearly understood that God would send someone to be their ruler (Micah 5:2) and king (Zechariah 9:9).

But what God told them and how they interpreted it didn't coincide. Living under Roman oppression, the Jews in Jesus's time envisioned their Messiah as a conquering king. One who would oust their oppressors and literally sit on a throne to rule over them. God, however, meant something entirely different. He wanted the Messiah to conquer sin for all people and to rule over their hearts and minds.

How could the Jews grasp this concept though? Their only examples of kings and rulers were embodied in human beings, such as King David, who fought physical battles and governed their day-to-day lives. Jesus's disciple Judas also struggled with this mental image versus the actions he observed Jesus take.

Today, with the benefit of hindsight and helpful Bible commentaries, Christians can see what God said about the Messiah being a Suffering Servant more than a man of military might. But perhaps what God is telling us now about other things is going over our heads. Just as the young adoptee concluded Miss Kitty was a cat, we might think we know what God means. Proverbs 3:5 advises against leaning on our own understanding. God's thoughts are not ours, so why not ask Him to open our eyes to what He is really saying to us?

Lesson Learned: What God says and how we interpret it may not be the same thing.

 Baby Steps to Growing Faith

1. Think of a time when you've misunderstood what someone said to you. Why were what you understood and what the speaker meant different?

2. How important is it to consider who is speaking to you and what their perspective is when you listen to the speaker's words?

3. Children don't always understand what adults tell them. Does that describe what happens to you as a child of your heavenly Father?

4. Before reading the Bible, say a prayer asking God to help you understand what He is saying. Afterward, consider whether that action made a difference.

Adventure 28

"I Had a Dream"

Once her baby was placed with adoptive parents, our office's contact with the birth mother typically ended. Occasionally a birth mother would reach out to us requesting we obtain pictures of and updates on her biological child to send her. Reading the information and seeing photo evidence of the adoptee's well-being we received always warmed my heart.

The result of one call from a birth mother making such a request, though, astounded us. The Boy Attorney spoke with this woman because I wasn't available, but he filled me in on their conversation.

"Do you know if the adoptive parents' house is near a field of yellow flowers?" the birth mother asked him.

"I'm really not sure," the Boy Attorney answered. "Why do you ask?"

The birth mother explained she'd been struggling a bit following the child's placement and wondering if her little one was OK. "But then I had a dream. I saw a field of beautiful yellow flowers near a house that I just knew was where my child lived. The scene made me feel like my child was OK and in a wonderful place. I need to find out if that's where she is."

Sensing the birth mother's great need for reassurance, my boss responded, "I honestly don't know what's near their house. But I can call the adoptive mother and find out. I'll also ask her to send us some pictures of the little one to pass along to you. That way you can see for yourself how your child is doing."

The birth mother thanked him profusely, relief evident in her voice.

Pulling the adoption file for this case, we found no mention of a field of flowers nearby in our clients' description of their home. Likewise, the adoption home study, which was detailed about the adoptive parents' home and community, failed to mention this landscape feature.

The Boy Attorney then called the adoptive mother with a surprising result.

"Do you have a field of yellow flowers near your house?" he inquired. "The birth mother dreamed her child now lives in a location with yellow flowers close by. She felt a sense of peace about that scene, and we want to reassure her all is well."

A stunned silence followed. The birth mother did not know the adoptive parents' identity or where they lived. How could she know what was near their house? Pulling herself together, the adoptive mother replied in the affirmative. Yes, sunflowers carpeted the field next to their house.

The adoptive mother mailed us photos of the child for the birth mother along with a picture of that yellow field. This gesture not only brought a smile to the birth mother's lips, but it brought her reassurance. Her child was well and being raised by loving people who even cared about the biological mother's peace of mind. The adoptive parents offered a bright and beautiful place to live. God made sure the birth mother received picture evidence of that fact. She did not need to worry.

Faith Lesson

> *The angel of God said to me in the dream, "Jacob." I answered, "Here I am." And he said, "Look up and see that all the male goats mating with the flock are streaked, speckled or spotted, for I have seen all that Laban has been doing to you. . . . Now leave this land at once and go back to your native land."*
>
> —Genesis 31:11–12, 13

From the beginning, God has been involved in the lives of the humans He created. Genesis 3:8 indicates that God came to the garden of Eden to walk with Adam and Eve. Walking with someone leads to conversation and closeness. The Creator wasn't an uninvolved, distant being. His connection with Adam and Eve was personal, and He kept an eye on what the two did. God knew when they slipped up and confronted them about it. Apple snack, anyone?

Likewise, God watched over Jacob in his daily life. Our heavenly Father knew full well Laban had been taking advantage of Jacob. But God didn't appear to Jacob live and in person as He did with Adam and Eve. Instead, God spoke to Jacob in a dream. He emphasized His awareness of Jacob's trying circumstances and provided him a way to extricate himself from that difficult situation: leave and return to his homeland.

A dream also pointed the way to the birth mother in this story to shed her doubts and fears about her placement decision and the well-being of her child. The scene in her dream of a beautiful field of yellow flowers prompted her to follow up with our office and to receive the reassurance and peace of mind she needed.

The connecting thread in these three situations is that God desires communication with us and may even initiate contact. We don't connect with Him only when we bow our heads or lift our hands. How He communicates with people may vary, and dreams may be one of those methods. Are you open to hearing from Him?

Lesson Learned: God communicates with us in various ways, including dreams.

 Baby Steps to Growing Faith

1. How does it make you feel to know God wants to communicate with you?

2. If God is everywhere, why wouldn't He be in your dreams?

3. Why would God choose a dream as a means of communication?

4. Have you ever had a dream you felt was a message from God? Why did you feel that dream was God communicating with you?

Adventure 29

What's in a Name?

Legally changing an adoptee's name to the one chosen by their adoptive parents is part of the adoption process. But before that point, the child has an original name. The birth mother may give the child a name she's selected, or she may decline to do so. In the latter case, the baby is typically known as Baby Boy or Baby Girl [birth mom's last name].

If the birth mother chooses to name the child, that name holds significance to her. Perhaps she names the child after a family member or a favorite character from a book or movie. Sometimes a name trending in society catches her fancy such as Nevaeh, which is *heaven* spelled backward.

But one name I read on a child's original birth certificate in an adoption case gave me pause. I'd never seen it before nor have I seen it since. What was it? Lady Stuffed Lion. [Well, something similar. I changed this name to protect privacy.] How in the world did the birth mother come up with that? I doubted a maternal relative bore that name, and I couldn't connect it to any popular name from movies, songs, or books.

Curiosity eventually got the better of me. The next time I spoke to the birth father, I asked about the baby's unusual name. As he explained, he and the birth mother, who had split up but remained friends, bought a stuffed lion for their baby during the pregnancy. The two lovingly spoke to their unborn child calling her "Lady Stuffed Lion."

The birth mother, who struggled with mental health issues, recognized her inability to parent her child. So, together with the birth father, she made the difficult decision, but the one she felt was best for her child, to place their baby for adoption. This woman poured love into the child she carried for the few months the two would share.

The hospital clerk who assisted the birth mother in filling out the child's birth certificate application may have raised an eyebrow at the name given. Likewise, staff at Florida's Office of Vital Statistics might have remarked, "Well, here's a name I haven't seen before!" But when I looked at the birth certificate knowing the story behind the name listed, it signified a mother's great and unselfish love for the child she carried but wouldn't be holding in the future.

Faith Lesson

> *For unto us a child is born, unto us a son is given: and the government shall be upon his shoulder: and his name shall be called Wonderful, Counsellor, The mighty God, The everlasting Father, The Prince of Peace.*
>
> —Isaiah 9:6 (KJV)

While the name Lady Stuffed Lion held great significance for the baby's parents in my adoption adventure, it also tells a story to those who hear it. No doubt exists that the biological parents loved their daughter. The two would only spend time with her as an unborn child and then very briefly following birth. The name they gave captured the essence of how they viewed her, a sweet bundle they could always love but could only care for during a fleeting bit of time.

Hundreds of years before the birth of Jesus, Isaiah referred to several names of a coming baby, the Messiah. And those names that the Old Testament prophet listed aptly describe Jesus and summarize His essence. He is wise, eternal, mighty, and a provider of peace.

Like Jesus, we also have more than one name. Our parents bestowed a name upon us when we were born. When we make the decision to follow Jesus, we also take on the name Christian. Our Savior's name is contained in the very word by which we are called. Do we live up to that name though? Are we Christlike? Do we act wisely? Focus on the eternal? Wield the power God offers? Sow His peace among those around us? Let's reflect the essence of our name Christian.

Lesson Learned: The names of God are significant.

 Baby Steps to Growing Faith

1. Do you know what your given first name means? If not, look it up. Does the name fit you?

2. Do people call you different names depending on the circumstances, such as a nickname by friends, a pet name by a significant

other? Does that explain why God might go by different names at different times?

3. Which of the names listed in Isaiah 9:6 do you think of most often as describing Jesus? Why?

4. Read Matthew 8:20; John 6:35; John 8:12; John 10:14; and John 14:6. By what names did Jesus refer to Himself?

Adventure 30

It Only Takes Once

If handling adoptions has taught me anything, it's that sex education needs to stress a key point: having sex *one time* can lead to pregnancy. While understanding the biological process is important, most people aren't thinking about science during moments of passion or lust. And even if they are, shouldn't the odds be in their favor? Well, do you want to take that chance? After my involvement in a shocking adoption case, I wouldn't.

The scenario appeared simple and straightforward from my brief initial phone conversation with the birth mother facing an unplanned pregnancy. She and the birth father lived together and were not ready to parent. They agreed an adoptive placement seemed the best option to pursue. So I scheduled a meeting in my office with the birth mother to discuss the adoption procedure and to complete the required background forms.

What a breath of fresh air! An easy case with a known and cooperative birth father. But I had a surprise in store for me.

When the birth mother came for her appointment with me, we enjoyed a pleasant conversation. She explained that she and the birth father had been together for five years. In the past few months, however, they'd experienced some difficulties and were trying to work on their relationship. A baby would simply add to the pressure they were under.

Then came the fateful question I always had to ask. "Is there any possibility that someone other than your boyfriend could be the baby's father?"

Waiting for the expected perfunctory negative answer, I heard the girl begin, "Well . . ." Her voice trailed off as she struggled to contain her emotions.

"I'm so sorry," I quickly said. "I don't mean to pry, but we have to make sure everything is done as Florida law requires so there won't be any problems with the adoption."

The girl nodded her head in understanding. "My boyfriend and I split up for a week. I was upset, so I went out drinking. I met a guy at the club, and we . . ." She failed to finish the sentence, but I didn't need words to grasp what had occurred.

With tears in her eyes, she looked at me and said, "But it was only one time. The baby has to be my boyfriend's. I don't know who the guy I met at the club was. I'd been drinking and can't remember much at all about that night."

"Does your boyfriend know about this encounter?" I asked.

"Yes, I told him as soon as we got back together. We had split up, so what could he say? But when I found out I was pregnant . . ."

"He doesn't want to raise a child that might possibly be someone else's, right?"

She looked down at her lap and nodded.

The adoption moved forward, and wonderful adoptive parents were selected to take placement of the baby. I provided them with background information on and the family medical history of the birth mother and her boyfriend. Our clients were also advised of the birth mother's one-time encounter. An unknown man could possibly be the child's biological father.

While this revelation did not deter our clients from proceeding, it did spur them to ask if a paternity test could be done solely so they would know if they had the biological father's medical and family history. The birth mother and her boyfriend agreed to the testing, which took place post-birth.

The mailman delivered the paternity test results to our office in a sealed envelope. The Boy Attorney stood at our receptionist's desk and opened it as I looked on. After glancing at the contents, he exclaimed, "I can't believe it! The unknown guy's the father. It only takes once!"

Faith Lesson

> *For Christ also suffered once for sins, the righteous for the unrighteous, to bring you to God. He was put to death in the body but made alive in the Spirit.*
>
> —1 Peter 3:18

Under the law of Moses, animal sacrifices atoned for the sins of the people. This practice was not a "one and done" thing. The practice only worked retroactively, for sins already committed. But, since man has a sinful nature, the priests repeatedly and endlessly slaughtered animals to atone for people's sins committed since the last sacrifice. Slaughtering animals could never provide perfect cleansing for sinners as Hebrews 10:10 states.

Meeting the requirements of Mosaic law resulted in the killing of thousands of animals (such as sheep, goats, and cows) and the shedding of a sea of blood. As an animal lover, I can't stand the thought. But the practice of animal sacrifice provides a point of comparison for what was to come: a better way to atone for sin.

The new way came in the person of Jesus. Yes, sacrifice and blood were involved, but it only took *one* time to atone for the sin of all—past, present, and future. Jesus, also known as the Lamb of God, sacrificed His life on the cross for me and for anyone else who accepts Him. Thankfully, no more animals need to die to make up for our misdeeds.

The paternity results in this adoption adventure determining that a one-time casual encounter led to the baby's conception stunned our office. But even more stunning? Jesus willingly endured a horrible death so that no further sacrifices need to be made to atone for my sins. In both cases, Jesus's death and the one-time sexual encounter, it only took once to provide a life-altering consequence.

Lesson Learned: Jesus died once for all time and for all people.

 Baby Steps to Growing Faith

1. Think of something you only get to do once in your life. Does the fact that it only occurs once make it more significant?

2. Would you take actions more deliberately if you knew an animal would be sacrificed if you made the wrong choice? Should the fact that Jesus was crucified, a cruel method of execution, to atone for

our sins be taken into account by believers when choosing between right and wrong actions?

3. Read Hebrews 10:9–10. Countless animal sacrifices were replaced by the sacrifice of Jesus's life, and Jesus died one time for all sins for all people for all time. What does that tell you about the power of God?

4. Read Hebrews 13:15. What's something that you should NOT do only once?

Adventure 31

"Help! He's Trying to Kill Me!"

"Birth mother Terri is on the line for you. She sounds upset and said she must speak with you immediately," our office's receptionist informed me.

What now? "Terri" had worked with our office on previous adoptive placements, and we knew her well. Her inability to stay off drugs kept getting her into difficult situations, including several unplanned pregnancies. We'd always been able to save the day when it came to making sure those babies found wonderful adoptive homes in which to grow up.

"Hi, Terri!" I said cheerfully.

But before I could utter another word, the birth mother screamed, "Help! He's trying to kill me!"

"Calm down, Terri," I replied in what I hoped was a soothing voice. "Who are you talking about?"

"My boyfriend. He's mad at me and has been chasing me all over the trailer park with a knife. He's trying to kill me."

"Where are you now?" I asked, thinking that the boyfriend was more likely acting crazy because he was high.

"I'm hiding in my trailer. Hopefully he won't find me."

Of course he won't. What would give him the idea she might be in her trailer? I shook my head and rolled my eyes.

"You've got to help me! Please!" she said with desperation in her voice.

"Terri, I'd love to help you, but I'm hours away from you in the Florida Panhandle, remember? I'm even in a different time zone. I can't really do anything to help you from here. If you're afraid your boyfriend might physically harm you, then call the police. They are in a better position to help you than I am."

"But I can't call the police," Terri wailed. "That would make him madder."

I refrained from pointing out that being alive was a higher priority than keeping her boyfriend from getting angrier. By this point in the conversation, I'd concluded that either Terri was herself high, and thus unlikely to be thinking clearly, or the boyfriend was her drug source, so she had to keep him around and not angry with her.

"Uh-oh," Terri gasped. "I think he's coming. I gotta go!"

I heard a click and then a dial tone.

Turning back to the work on my desk, it was hard not to think about the scene in a trailer park in Central Florida where a scared pregnant woman was being pursued by an angry and possibly high man with a knife. I lifted a prayer for her safety. *Heaven help her because I can't at this moment.* And God answered my request by keeping Terri safe.

Faith Lesson

> *I lift up my eyes to the mountains—*
> *where does my help come from?*
> *My help comes from the LORD,*
> *the Maker of heaven and earth.*
>
> —Psalm 121:1–2

Finding the right person in your time of need is important. Don't call me if your car requires repair work. I wouldn't have a clue what to do. But if you have a question about adoption, I'm your gal. While no one person can effectively help with every problem you might encounter, God can. If He can make heaven and earth as noted in Psalm 121:2, we know we can count on His ability to help.

The hitch is that we must ask God for His assistance. And Matthew 7:7 assures us that if we ask, we will receive. So, why don't we? Does God not spring to mind when we're in trouble? It does to "foxhole Christians," who turn to Him in desperation. Why wouldn't a believer think of their heavenly Father first when the going gets tough? Does pride make us think we can deal with the situation on our own? That's courting disaster since the Bible indicates pride precedes destruction (Proverbs 16:18).

The terrified birth mother in this story calling me for help emphasizes to me the need to ascertain who your best helper is. The answer is simple. It's always God.

Lesson Learned: Look to the right place for help: to God.

 Baby Steps to Growing Faith

1. When you have a problem, who is the first person you turn to for help? Why do you look to that person?

2. List three reasons why someone may not be able to help you. Would any of those reasons keep God from helping you?

3. Read Psalm 46:1. When is God available to help you?

4. If you knew someone had the ability and willingness to help you, wouldn't you seek his or her assistance? List a reason why you don't turn to God. Is that a good reason?

Adventure 32

Disturbing Darkness

The dark sky above me and the rumbling of thunder made for a gloomy drive to the jail in another county. My assignment was to meet with a birth father and discuss the birth mother's proposed adoptive placement. I had no qualms about trips to courthouses and hospitals, but spending time in a correctional facility didn't rate in the top ten places this adoption attorney wanted to go for work-related tasks. And the bad weather didn't help.

As I arrived at the facility, the heavens opened, and rain poured down. At that point, the jail facility offered one positive—shelter from the elements. Claps of thunder boomed while I showed my attorney ID to the desk sergeant and obtained clearance to meet with the birth father. He pointed me to the door leading to where the inmates were held. The officer's parting words? "Whatever you do, don't let the prisoner keep a pen or a paper clip. It can be used as a weapon in here." If I hadn't been nervous before, I certainly was then.

Stepping inside where I'd been directed, I heard a click as the door locked behind me. Ahead of me was a similar door, one that the officer who cleared me would have to remotely unlock to allow my further progress. As my shoulders and neck tensed, the unthinkable happened. With a tremendous boom, the power in the facility went out. I was stranded in the dark inside a men's jail.

While the loss of power scared me, it energized the inmates. Whooping, screaming, and whistling assaulted my ears. I fervently prayed my location would remain secure despite the power outage. Before I could totally freak out, power came back on. Thank heaven for an emergency generator!

The door ahead of me made a clicking sound and unlocked. I stepped out of the small area in which I'd been trapped. A corrections officer met me and escorted me to the attorney-prisoner conference room. Did he say room? The area I entered could have passed for a broom closet. Four bare walls, one with a small window in which the guard outside could occasionally peek to check on my safety, surrounded me. Two chairs and a small table filled the cramped space. I'd moved from physical darkness in the entry during a power outage to figurative darkness in a controlled area of a jail.

Enter the birth father. He was friendly and chatty. Well, of course. He was out of his cell doing something different and talking to someone new. After explaining the purpose for my visit, I pulled out the forms I needed him to review and sign. I stifled a gasp as I realized paper clips held the forms together. Would it be too obvious to take them off and put them aside where he couldn't reach them? The prisoner picked up a form and slyly removed the paper clip, quickly inserting it into one of his socks. What could I do?

Next, with trepidation, I passed a pen to him to use to sign the form. I could've shouted for joy when he handed it back along with the form now bearing his signature. Whew!

My business completed, I wanted out of there. But the birth father continued chatting. He felt like shooting the breeze. What else did he have to do? To humor him, I carried on a conversation for a bit. Not doing so might make him angry and, well, he had a paper clip in his possession. Sure, I had a pen for protection, but I didn't want to push my luck.

Finally, I gathered the courage to say I had to leave, emphasizing it was a long way back to my office and driving would be slow in the bad weather. Catching the guard's attention, I hastily departed the claustrophobic conference room.

Safely back in my car, I began my return trip. Tension still gripped me though. Would I hear on the news the next day that a prisoner had died at the jail, the victim of a paper clip attack? Thankfully, that scenario never occurred, but I still wasn't eager to return to the correctional facility, with or without paper clips in my file and even if the power stayed on.

Faith Lesson

> *At noon, darkness came over the whole land until three in the afternoon. And at three in the afternoon Jesus cried out in a loud voice, "Eloi, Eloi, lema sabachthani?" (which means "My God, my God, why have you forsaken me?").*
> —Mark 15:33–34

The total darkness enveloping me as I was stuck in the passage between the jail lobby and the jail's interior shook me. Without light, I couldn't see the doors or the walls or determine if an intercom existed. I was totally helpless.

Being in such pervasive darkness is nothing any of us would choose to do for an extended time. But Jesus willingly made that choice when He died to provide salvation for those who would accept Him. The Light of the World had His very life extinguished and suffered excruciating darkness and separation from our heavenly Father because He loved us so much.

Literal darkness covered the land for the three hours prior to Jesus's death on the cross as detailed in Matthew 27:45 and Mark 15:33. Even worse, He agonized at the darkness of His heavenly Father turning His back on Him while Jesus took on our sins. And the darkness continued upon removal of Jesus's body from the cross. No light could touch His body as it was wrapped in a clean cloth, placed inside a tomb cut into the rock, and covered with a huge stone.

But Sunday morning, the sun rose and brought light into the world as Jesus rose and brought the Light of the World out of that dark tomb. Now His light again shines here in a dark sinful world.

The darkness I experienced while trapped in a correctional facility's small passageway during a power outage was disturbing. What counteracted the fear produced? The lights coming back on. Jesus, who has been through disturbing darkness Himself, offers us light in our lives. Not just any light, but the Light of the World. Why stay in disturbing darkness? Go to the Light!

Lesson Learned: Jesus endured great darkness by His death for me.

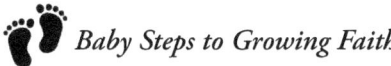 *Baby Steps to Growing Faith*

1. Darkness is the opposite of light. Why is that difference important to remember?

2. Identify three things that bring "darkness" into your life.

3. To get rid of darkness in your house, you rely on the energy of lamps. How do you get rid of darkness in your spiritual life? On what Light can you rely?

4. Read John 8:12. Where are you walking today? Why?

Adventure 33

"You Ain't Gettin' on This Base!"

With an office located only five minutes from the gate of Eglin Air Force Base, we often handled adoptions involving military personnel and their dependents. And since the military provided health care, a large base hospital served the military population. Birth mothers would sometimes deliver at the facility, requiring arrangements to be made for nonmilitary prospective adoptive parents to gain access to the base to get to the hospital.

Being a military "dependent," I had access to the base with my military ID card. I could freely come and go to the base hospital on adoption business. But getting clients without an ID through the guarded gate was a process involving paperwork at the visitor's center. They had to obtain a visitor's pass. And not just anybody could obtain such a pass. Someone with a valid military ID needed to vouch for them.

One morning I met my clients, a wonderful young couple, at my office to travel to Eglin's hospital to meet their newly born family member. The birth mother insisted the couple come and spend time with the baby prior to the child's discharge. Of course, the husband and wife were thrilled at the prospect of being with the baby, but they were on edge about a possible meeting with the birth mother. On top of that concern, I could tell they were nervous about entering a military installation since they had no military connection.

To ease their anxiety, I explained the process to them. "It's very straightforward. We park at the visitor's center just before the gate where the guards stand." I elected to omit that the guards were visibly armed, and not just with small handguns. "We'll go into the visitor's center," I continued, "where I'll show them my ID, you'll produce your driver's licenses, some paperwork will be filled out, and you'll be handed a pass to show to the gate guards to access the base. It shouldn't take long, especially since today's a federal holiday. Only essential base personnel are working."

Access to the base is restricted to military ID holders or those sponsored by one.

The clients followed me to the base in their car, meeting me in the visitor's center parking lot. Little traffic was on the road, and the parking lot itself was almost completely empty.

Entering the small building, we observed only one service member in the office. Seated behind a desk facing the front door, she was talking to someone else seeking a visitor's pass. We stepped off to the side to allow her to complete that task, but we couldn't help overhearing the ongoing conversation.

"Sir, I understand you have a picture ID and have a business reason to be on the base. However, for me to issue a visitor's pass, you must have someone with an ID who can vouch for you."

"Oh, I know plenty of people who have IDs and access to the base," the man responded.

"But can they come and show me their ID and vouch for you so I can issue you a pass?"

"Can't you just talk to them on the phone? These are people who work here and are on base all the time."

Glancing at the prospective adoptive father, I noticed his widened eyes. I gathered he was getting nervous security was so tight that he and his wife might be denied access to the base. I flashed him a reassuring smile, but it didn't seem to help.

The conversation between the military member and the would-be entrant continued, but it went round and round. Despite the clear message given by the woman behind the desk, the man persisted in trying to get a pass without a sponsor present.

Finally, the woman reached her breaking point. "*Sir*, do you have someone with an ID who will come to this building and vouch for you right now? If not, you ain't gettin' on this base!"

My clients and I stifled giggles. The man got the message at last and left without a pass. The military member then smiled at me as I stepped forward with my military ID in hand and the couple behind me with their driver's licenses at the ready. I explained we were headed to the hospital for them to meet the baby they would be adopting. She was as polite and professional as could be and quickly prepared the required visitors' pass for them. We *were* gettin' on that base!

Faith Lesson

> *Jesus answered, "I am the way and the truth and the life. No one comes to the Father except through me."*
>
> —John 14:6

Technology offers drivers various routes to get to a specific location. Options include the most direct route, the route that avoids major traffic points, or one staying on the main roads. The driver selects which way to go to reach their intended destination, but all options lead him there.

Having a plethora of travel options is good because people have choices. But this situation is bad in that they become accustomed to choosing and expect to do so all the time. Take the man trying to access the military installation in my adoption adventure. The base offered only one way for a non-ID holder to obtain a visitor's pass. Someone with an ID had to appear and vouch for them. That didn't sit well with this man, and it was inconvenient since he didn't have an ID holder handy to assist him.

Access to our heavenly Father is similarly restricted. Jesus made clear to His disciples that only through Him could they get to the Father. He is "the" way—the one and only way. He stands ready to vouch for each of us who accept Him and follow Him. Without Him? Well, you ain't gettin' to the Father!

Lesson Learned: Jesus is our sponsor for gaining access to our Father in heaven, and the only way to obtain it.

Baby Steps to Growing Faith

1. Think of a time when you had to show something like a ticket to gain access to a venue, perhaps a movie theater or a sporting event. Did you make sure you had that ticket with you when trying to enter the venue? Would you have gotten in without it?

2. Imagine you had the opportunity to meet the president of the United States at the White House. Would you enter the door where you were directed, or would you try to gain access at another point? Is accessing God any different?

3. What's more important to you: being with your heavenly Father or having control over how to get there?

4. Read John 14:6 aloud. Is there any ambiguity in what Jesus said about how to come to the Father?

Adventure 34

"Why Are Those People Looking at Me?"

The stress in the nurse's voice came through loud and clear during our phone conversation. She, as well as all the other nurses on duty in the hospital's maternity area, couldn't wait for this patient, a birth mother I was working with, to get out of there. While the nurse remained professional and did not use those exact words, the sentiment was obvious. The patient drove them all crazy.

Unfortunately, the birth mother's behavior stemmed from doing the right thing. Since she suffered from mental health issues, her doctor prescribed medication to control them. When she took those medications, she could function on a more even keel. But taking them during pregnancy was not recommended. The birth mother voiced a concern about doing anything that might harm her unborn child. So, she made a firm decision not to take those pills while pregnant.

The results of this decision? Protection for her baby but a mental and emotional roller coaster for her. And things weren't always so wonderful for those around her who experienced her erratic and difficult behavior. Even worse? Following delivery, birth mothers experience a surge of hormones. My boss called this situation a "hormone hurricane."

The poor nurses attending maternity patients were run ragged by this birth mother's constant demands and poorly controlled emotions. The staff didn't deal with patients with mental conditions on a regular basis, and after this patient, they sure didn't want to in the future. The staff knew the consent to adoption had to be signed before the woman's discharge. When could I get there? I tactfully explained I had to observe the Florida law's requisite waiting time to take the consent. It was a long forty-eight hours after delivery for these nurses.

Finally, the authorized time came, and I arrived at the hospital with two witnesses. Why witnesses? Someone must confirm the paperwork was signed voluntarily, no promises were made to induce the birth mother to sign, and the birth mother understood what was occurring. I provided this explanation to the birth mother in front of the witnesses and a couple of nurses who were in the room.

As I placed my stack of legal paperwork on her tray table, all of which had been sent to the birth mother in advance for review, I sensed this process was going to get bumpy. Sadly, my fears were confirmed. The first piece of paper I handed to her for signature, a standard medical release, upset her for some reason.

She kept asking why she had to sign it, and I gave the simplest explanation I could. "We must have your permission to obtain medical records on you and the baby from the hospital so the adoptive parents' pediatrician has the information needed to care for the baby."

After I went back and forth a bit with the poor girl, her attending nurse spoke up. With just a trace of irritation in her voice she said, "That's the form the federal government requires be signed. The law is HIPAA. Everyone has to sign the form, and it's a standard form." Finally, the birth mother saw the light and put her signature on the form.

Whew! Just forty-five pages or so to go, I thought gloomily.

As I went through the paperwork to be signed, the birth mother kept glancing over and glaring at the two witnesses seated on a small couch against the wall facing her hospital bed. Finally, she interrupted me and growled, "Why are those people looking at me?"

I could tell the nurse beside me wanted to slap her forehead. Instead, she said in as controlled a voice as she could manage, "Remember, Alice told you the law says she must have two witnesses here to make sure everything is done correctly? They're here to look out for *you*."

The nurse's explanation hit home with the patient, and we continued with signing the paperwork. It was one of the longest and most difficult consent signings in my career. But it was also one of the most inspiring. What love that birth mother had for her child to go without medication that would have made her life more bearable! I so admired her. And I hoped all the other people looking at her in the room felt the same way.

Faith Lesson

> *But if they will not listen, take one or two others along, so that "every matter may be established by the testimony of two or three witnesses."*
>
> —Matthew 18:16

In Old Testament times (Deuteronomy 19:15) and when Jesus was alive, the Jews recognized the necessity of two to three witnesses to establish any matter. Laws today also require witnesses. The witnesses are needed to establish the circumstances surrounding the execution of a document such as a will or a consent to adoption, for example. They can attest that the person signing the document was acting voluntarily and understood what they were signing. The witnesses' testimony provides evidence of the document's validity.

What makes up legal documents? They consist of words. John 1:1 tells us the ultimate Word is God. And, as John 1:14 (KJV) states, the Word became flesh and "dwelt among us." During Jesus's ministry on earth, disciples surrounded Him. At all times He had witnesses to attest not only to His teachings but also to His mighty works. Ultimately, the disciples were witnesses about Jesus and who He was.

Jesus is not physically on earth now, but witnesses are still needed to attest to what He has done. Praying with fellow believers, for example, is a way to observe Jesus at work. The answer to prayer can be seen, and God's response may be established by witnesses. You can only talk about what you see, and that's why people are led to look to Him. Are you serving as a witness?

Lesson Learned: Witnesses play an important role in establishing what happened.

Baby Steps to Growing Faith

1. Think of something you have witnessed God do in the life of someone you know. How would you describe it if called as a witness about the situation?

2. Does having more than one person agree on what God has done in someone's life make it more believable? If so, why?

3. Do you feel more comfortable sharing what has happened if another witness can attest to the same thing? Why would that be?

4. Is a witness's testimony less believable if it varies on some details from that of another witness? Why or why not?

Adventure 35

Poker Face

"They just signed the discharge papers, so I can leave the hospital," the birth mother informed me over the phone. "How soon can you be here to do the adoption paperwork with me? I want to get out of here!"

"I know you do, and I'll be there as quickly as I can, but it's over an hour's drive to the hospital from my office," I responded. "Let me grab my two witnesses and the paperwork for you to sign, and we'll head your way."

"Please, get here as soon as you can. I really want to go home."

"I understand, and I'll do what I can. You know how traffic can be." Hopefully knowing I was on the way would keep the poor girl pacified until I could get to the hospital.

Some two hours later, I finally arrived and checked with the medical staff. "The birth mother is very anxious to see you so she can get her paperwork signed and then leave," a nurse told me.

Her assessment proved spot on. I headed toward the birth mother's room with the two witnesses trailing behind me like baby ducks following their mother. Then I spotted her. She was pacing up and down the hallway outside her room.

"Oh, *there* you are!" she exclaimed breathlessly. "I've been waiting!"

"Here I am with the witnesses and the paperwork," I said pointing to both. "Let's get this done so you can go home." But before I could get into her room, the birth mother stopped me.

"There is one thing I, well, we, needed to ask you." The birth father came out of her hospital room and stood beside the birth mother, both facing me.

Nervously, the birth mother looked at me and said, "I've been thinking."

Uh-oh. Here we go.

"The adoptive parents have been really nice to help me with my rent and utilities while I was pregnant. But so I can get on my feet, I was thinking they could help me go to beauty school. Then I could support myself."

Before responding, I turned to the witnesses and asked them to step over and sit in the nearby waiting area. "I need to talk to the birth parents before we can do the paperwork," I explained.

Then I faced the birth mother. "I know the adoptive parents would love to help you if they could. Unfortunately, Florida law doesn't allow them to pay for that type of expense."

Until this point, the birth father had merely stood there not saying a word. But he piped up at this point to exclaim, "But she's giving them her *baby*. Shouldn't she get something out of it?"

Taking a breath, I calmly and professionally pointed out she was getting a wonderful life for her child with a stable and loving couple. Her child would have all her needs met. "But regardless, Florida law will not authorize the adoptive parents to pay for that training."

"Nobody has to know," the birth father persisted.

"Actually, they do. We are required to file an affidavit, which is a sworn statement, with the court listing all expenses the couple paid connected to the adoption. We cannot lie."

The birth father clenched his jaws and glared at me. The birth mother remained quiet, giving me the distinct impression the idea for this request for additional financial assistance came from him.

"I'm sure plenty of couples would be happy to pay for her schooling if they got a baby girl," he spat out.

"Perhaps there are. She is free to place her child through our office if she wants or she can find another couple. However, if we make the placement, we will follow the law and cannot help her financially with beauty school training. If she does not want to place through us, I will leave, but I don't think you'll be able to find someone quickly enough that you can go home from the hospital without the baby today. You might have to take her home for a few days before other arrangements can be made through another adoption office."

Although the words came out in a controlled manner, my brain was about to explode. My knees wobbled a bit. Could I just turn around and leave if the birth parents pushed back? That was the only option. And how would I explain that outcome to the couple awaiting the baby's placement with them later than afternoon?

My remark about having to take the baby home for a few days apparently hit home with the birth father. He backed down, and the birth mother indicated she wanted to proceed with signing the adoption paperwork.

"I'll meet you in the hospital room. Let me go get my witnesses."

The wide eyes of my two witnesses revealed they had overhead the encounter. "Oh, my! I couldn't believe you told them you could just leave," one said. "You looked so calm and collected. I couldn't have done that."

"If I'd been wearing boots, I would've been shaking in them," I responded with a relieved smile.

"You'd never have known it," the witness said. "What a poker face!"

Faith Lesson

> *But we Christians have no veil over our faces; we can be mirrors that brightly reflect the glory of the Lord. And as the Spirit of the Lord works within us, we become more and more like him.*
>
> —2 Corinthians 3:18 (TLB)

While I'm not a poker player, I understand the concept of displaying a poker face. You don't want fellow card players to know whether you have a good hand or a bad one. It's a strategic move. Applied to situations outside of card games, the term describes a face that does not reveal what an individual is thinking or feeling.

When dealing with the birth mother in my adoption adventure, I did not want her to sense I was concerned things would fall through if I didn't accede to her request for additional financial assistance. Why? Because understanding my worry might have fueled her resolve to press for more money. I had to zealously represent and protect my clients, so a poker face was the correct move to make.

But with our faith life, Jesus wants people to clearly see His followers' thoughts and feelings about Him. A poker face does not advance the Great Commission's aim to disciple the world. The peace, hope, and love being a Christian brings should be evident on our faces to nonbelievers. How evident? The apostle Paul notes in 2 Corinthians 3:18 that we should "brightly reflect" the Lord's glory.

While playing cards, keeping mum about a surprise birthday party, or appearing confident in a nerve-wracking job interview, a poker face is appropriate. But clearly reflecting the light and love of Jesus is a believer's goal when interacting with others. Don't let a poker face dim that reflection.

Lesson Learned: Our face should clearly reflect the image of our heavenly Father.

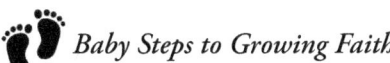
Baby Steps to Growing Faith

1. Your face is usually the first thing seen when you are introduced to someone. Based on your face alone, what would they conclude about you if they met you right now? Are you blessed? Hopeful? Other?

2. If you met another Christian, what would you expect to see in their face?

3. Right before my mother's death, she had a new nurse take a shift to care for her at the hospital. When the woman walked into the room, Mom looked at her face and said, "You know Jesus, don't you?" What do you think Mom saw to tell her that?

4. Read Numbers 6:25. If we are to reflect God to others, how can we make our face "shine" to catch the attention of nonbelievers? Identify and put into practice one idea for a "shinier" face.

Adventure 36

Spitting Image

When a nonrelative adopts, no biological connection exists between parent and child. The law, however, gives legal recognition to their family relationship. A court document confirms they are family, but a physical similarity between the two is unlikely since no DNA is shared.

The judge sees the parents and child at the final adoption hearing. On numerous occasions, judges have emphasized how such hearings are the only real bright spot in their daily court docket. Everyone leaves smiling or if they are crying, it is tears of joy. While a judge observes the family's joy, they rarely see a physical resemblance between the adoptee and his or her new parents.

One hearing I handled proved to be the exception rather than the rule. As usual, we assembled in the judge's chambers, the fancy term for his office. A conference table against the front of the judge's desk extended out to form a T. I sat on the left side of the table directly across from my beaming clients. The husband held a baby boy on his lap. Adorably dressed up and in a good mood, the little one smiled and cooed.

The judge directed me to begin my presentation and questioning of the husband and wife. By this point in the court proceedings, all required reports and paperwork had been submitted and the necessary approvals obtained. The hearing was basically a formality, but a very important one since the adoption would be legally finalized.

As I proceeded with my usual checklist of questions, I observed that the judge wasn't paying attention to what I said. Instead, he looked back and forth between the child and the soon-to-be legal father like watching a tennis match. The judge's scrutiny was so intense I probably could have asked the husband if he'd eaten a peanut butter and jelly sandwich for lunch, and the judge wouldn't have noticed.

When I concluded, the judge failed to announce that the adoption was approved. He merely stated, "I can't believe the adoptee and the father aren't biologically related. They look so much alike!" As if needing confirmation of this conclusion, he turned to his bailiff and asked. "Don't you think they look alike?" Of course, the bailiff agreed. It was true, but the court officer wouldn't have disagreed with the judge even if the man and child looked nothing alike. My clients and I also nodded in agreement.

Additional gazing back and forth continued until I finally spoke up and prompted conclusion of the hearing by telling the judge I had a proposed Final Judgment of Adoption for his signature. With a stroke of his pen, the judge created a legal parent-child relationship between my clients and the baby. As we departed the judge's chambers, a discussion continued between the judge and the bailiff about the child's striking resemblance to the adoptive father. Resemblance or not, the two were now legally related, and I could prove it with the newly signed Final Judgment of Adoption in my hand.

Faith Lesson

> *If you really know me, you will know my Father as well. From now on, you do know him and have seen him. . . . Anyone who has seen me has seen the Father. How can you say, "Show us the Father"?*
>
> —John 14:7, 9

Faith requires much from Christians. They must believe in God even though they've never seen Him. Even the disciples faced this challenge. Accordingly, Philip asked Jesus to show them the Father (John 14:8).

Perhaps with a bit of irritation, Jesus explained such action was unnecessary. The disciples had, in fact, seen His Father. How? Because they had seen Jesus, the spitting image of His Father. Jesus served as the embodiment of God on this earth. The characteristics He displayed, such as love and compassion for the outcasts of society, and the power He displayed through numerous miracles performed spoke volumes about who God is and what He can do.

But, if Jesus no longer walks this earth, how can people today know God? The light of Jesus shines in every one of His followers, although brighter in some than in others. Nonbelievers can know about God through what they observe in and about those carrying the light of Jesus in their life. For this reason, Jesus emphasized in Matthew 5:16 that believers should let our light so shine before others that God will be glorified.

Galatians 4:4–5 states God has adopted believers as His children through Jesus's redemption. Don't Christians want to display that relationship through their resemblance to their heavenly Father?

What a witness to the world it would be if we were the spitting image of our Father. Let's capture the attention of those around us with that resemblance just as the child's resemblance to his adoptive father transfixed the presiding judge.

Lesson Learned: I should resemble my heavenly Father.

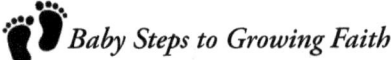 *Baby Steps to Growing Faith*

1. Identify four ways Jesus resembled His heavenly Father.

2. What would a nonbeliever think God is like based on observing you?

3. Who do you know that embodies a clear image of God through their Christian walk?

4. What is something specific you can do toward becoming a spitting image of God?

Adventure 37

Bond, Jane Bond

The mission I chose to accept involved meeting a birth mother in a neighboring county. She wanted to talk to me in person to obtain information about the option of placing her baby for adoption. Her family would not be supportive of this decision, so she made clear that her interactions with me must be kept in the strictest confidence.

"Where would you like to meet?" I asked her over the phone. "I assume your house would not be a good choice under the current circumstances."

"No, let's meet at the park," she suggested, giving me the name of the park and an idea of its location.

After nailing down the meeting spot and time, the birth mother added to the plan. "When you arrive, sit at a picnic table, and let *me* come to you. Don't approach me. If I see someone who knows me, I won't come over. I'd probably leave and then call you to coordinate a different meeting time."

I, of course, agreed to her instructions. But inwardly I sighed. The birth mother lived in a small town. The odds were high she'd see someone she knew or someone she knew would see her. *Oh well, at least I'm being paid to drive an hour each way to the agreed upon location if this meeting falls through.*

And an added step for security? The pregnant girl asked me to wear something casual. Something one would wear to a park and not to the office. I understood. Hanging out in a dress, hose, and heels in a park in a small rural town would be out of place and draw attention. No problem.

The day of the meeting arrived, and I called to confirm our plans before leaving my office. I assured the girl I was attired in casual clothes and would await her joining me at a picnic table at the designated meeting location. I felt the urge to ask the birth mother if she wanted to synchronize watches, but I thought that might be too flip a comment and refrained.

While driving to the park, I reviewed the situation in my mind. *Too bad I don't have a trench coat to wear. But wearing sunglasses might not be a bad idea. Remember to check the area to see if anyone's there before leaving the car. What if someone approaches me and asks what I'm doing there when I'm with the birth mother? What should I say?*

Upon arrival, I carefully surveyed the premises before leaving my car. No one was in sight, including the birth mother. But then, I always show up early, so her absence at that point was not concerning. Sitting down at a picnic table with a view of the road leading to the park, I awaited her arrival. From time to time, I'd hear a car and jump, but then I'd try to appear nonchalant.

Finally, the birth mother showed up. I refrained from looking at her in case someone was watching me from somewhere. The girl scoped out the area. Satisfied the two of us had the park to ourselves, she approached me. We talked at length about her current situation, the options available to her, and what the adoption process was like. But the whole time, I was on pins and needles waiting for the two of us to be exposed. Fortunately, none of her family members or friends happened upon us, and no foreign agents appeared out of the woodwork. Whew!

Mission accomplished, I got in my vehicle (not an Aston Martin) and drove back to the office to report to B (my boss). This meeting firmly convinced me that cloak-and-dagger stuff is much more fun when you are watching James Bond do it on the silver screen. I don't have any desire to be Bond, Jane Bond.

Faith Lesson

> *Can any hide himself in secret places that I shall not see him? saith the* LORD*. Do not I fill heaven and earth? saith the* LORD*.*
>
> —Jeremiah 23:24 (KJV)

Attempts to hide date back to the beginning of recorded history. Genesis relates that Adam and Eve naively decided to hide from God in the garden of Eden. Later, the Bible tells of Jonah sailing off in the opposite direction than God had directed, attempting to escape from Him. But God found all of them.

Hiding can sometimes be fun. Greek writers record children playing a type of hide-and-seek game in that ancient civilization. And today kids still enjoy hiding from "It," who is tasked with finding them.

In a more serious vein, adults often try to hide things such as addictions, affairs, and criminal behavior. In my adoption adventure, the birth mother sought to conceal her meeting with me. While people may succeed in hiding information from others, they cannot do so with God. The Creator is everywhere. He points out in Jeremiah 23:24 that no hiding place exists in which He cannot see us.

Our attempts to cover things up are like the young child who hides behind a curtain with his feet sticking out. He thinks he's found a clever hiding place, but his parents can easily spot him. Likewise, hiding from Father God is futile. He is the "It" who will never fail to find you.

Lesson Learned: You can't hide from God.

 Baby Steps to Growing Faith

1. Were Adam, Eve, and Jonah compounding their difficulties by trying to hide from God? If so, how?

2. Think of one thing about yourself that you hide from others. How do you feel knowing God sees what you have hidden?

3. Is the awareness that you can't hide anything from God something that can help you hold yourself accountable for what you do, say, and think?

4. Would you still want to hide from God if you knew He loved you regardless of what you've done? If you knew He'd forgive you if you simply asked? Read 1 John 1:9.

Adventure 38

"Gypsies, Tramps, and Thieves"

My earliest memory of the term *Gypsy* is from an elementary school class party. The fun included not only sweet treats but a chance to win prizes. The most coveted prize by far was a record of Cher's hit single, "Gypsies, Tramps, and Thieves." The song's lyrics made clear that people didn't hold Gypsies in high regard.

Although I knew about the existence of Gypsies since childhood, I never met a Gypsy until I was an adult. A social worker called me about a concerning case on which she'd been working. Under the circumstances, she believed an adoptive placement would be best for all concerned. The child, who was back in the hospital, suffered from physical issues related to a disability present at birth.

The social worker and I spoke at length about the details of the situation. Two things she told me gave me a jolt. First, the birth mother was a Gypsy. *What is a Gypsy doing in the US and particularly in Florida? Don't they live in Romania and Hungary or at least somewhere in Europe?*

A second jolt resulted from the reason for the placement. The family, who earned a living by fortune-telling, believed a curse had caused the child's medical issues. *A curse? In this day and age?*

Intrigued, I did some research about Gypsies and learned the Romani or Roma are a mainly ethnic group of traditionally itinerant people[6] who originated in northern India.[7] While Gypsies can still be found in Europe today, over one million people in the US are of Romani ancestry.[8] I also learned that Roma generally view the term *Gypsy* as a racial slur.[9] Good thing I found that out before talking with the birth mother and misspoke.

As part of the placement process, I met with the birth mother in my office. She made a striking appearance with her dark skin and dark eyes.

Florida law required me to obtain various information for background forms, including her motivation for making an adoptive placement. Taking an inward deep breath, I forged ahead. *And here we go.*

"Can you tell me why you are considering placing your child for adoption?"

"This child suffers because of a curse placed on him before birth. A curse relates to evil, and we must remove evil from our family," she matter-of-factly explained. Her controlled voice bore no hint of emotion. The box of tissues placed strategically on the corner of my desk near her went unused.

---

[6] "Gypsies by State 2024," World Population Review, https://worldpopulationreview.com/state-rankings/gypsies-by-state, accessed August 16, 2024.

[7] Ian F. Hancock, "Romani Americans (Roma)," Texas State Historical Association, December 1, 1995, https://www.tshaonline.org/handbook/entries/roma-gypsies.

[8] Hancock, "Romani Americans (Roma)."

[9] "Gypsies by State 2024."

If the words straight from her mouth weren't enough to convince me, the look in her eyes did. She honestly believed a curse was in place, and evil threatened her family. Prior to this meeting, I'd briefly considered that her choosing adoption might have been based on the difficulty of caring for a disabled child. But that reason, if indeed a factor, served only as an afterthought. The belief a curse existed undeniably motivated the birth mother's placement decision.

Yes, evil was present in this situation, but not in the way the birth mother thought. The act of uttering words to place (or at least attempt to place) a curse on an innocent unborn child was simply evil. And those evil words caused the destruction of a family. How sad.

Faith Lesson

> *But no human being can tame the tongue. It is a restless evil, full of deadly poison.*
>
> —James 3:8

It's happened to all of us. We thoughtlessly blurt out words that wound someone else. Although a child might say "Take that back!" it's too late. The damage has already been done. Even if you apologize, the memory of the words is seared into the brain of the one at whom they were directed. You can take the nail out of the piece of wood, but the hole remains.

To counter thoughtless words requires thought. The usual advice is to think before you speak. Better yet, pray for God's assistance before arriving at a situation where the temptation to speak evil might overtake you. Does a coworker really get your goat? Pray prior to going to work, when irritation and anger aren't at play, for help with tongue control in the heat of the moment.

More puzzling to me than thoughtless words are those words spoken to harm someone. Think of intentionally blaming a person for a crime they didn't commit or of lying about someone that could result in their firing. Serious negative consequences could result from such calculated words.

The curse spoken in this adoption adventure falls into such a category. Whether the person's curse caused the child's handicap isn't the point. But those words sowed a seed of fear and doubt into the family's mind. Ultimately, it caused the family's destruction when an adoption took place because the child no longer had legal ties to his biological relatives.

The words of the curse were a deadly poison as James 3:8 describes the evil words the tongue speaks. They affected not just the birth mother, who was told her child had been cursed, but her entire family and, saddest of all, an innocent child.

I don't want to spread lethal poison whether unintentionally or by calculation. Let's practice poison control with God's help. Tame the tongue!

Lesson Learned: Using the tongue can produce much evil.

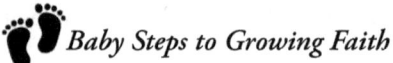
Baby Steps to Growing Faith

1. Is God only concerned about believers' actions, or does He care about their words as well? Are you loving your neighbor when you say hurtful things to them or to others about them?

2. Think of a time when you said something hurtful to another person. Was your tongue "tamed" (under control) when you uttered those words? If not, what might you have said if it had been?

3. *Taming* means to subdue or master. It's understandable that taming a wild horse would be difficult, but why is it so much trouble to tame something as small as your tongue?

4. What's one practical step you can take to tame your tongue?

Adventure 39

Asked and Answered

Years back when a newspaper was a tangible item you held in your hands to read rather than viewing online, classified ads were popular. Want to find a roommate? Run a classified ad. Looking for a new employee? Run a classified ad. Wish to adopt a baby? Run a classified ad. Wait, what? Yes. Florida law allows prospective adoptive parents to advertise their desire to adopt, but they must do so through a licensed attorney. Does that method work? Well, in one instance it literally worked miraculously.

"To be honest," I told the prospective adoptive couple, "almost all the children our office places are newborns directly from the hospital. Toddlers and older children are usually adopted out of the state foster care system. We can keep our eyes open for a two-year-old for you, but that would be an unusual situation."

Despite my frank assessment, the couple remained undeterred in working with us to fulfill their desire to adopt a two-year-old. "What could we do to increase our chances of finding a child of that age?" they asked me.

I explained how running an ad expressing interest in adopting a young child was an option. However, I cautioned that placing such ads did not guarantee a child could be located. Pursuing the option would also involve payment of publication expenses.

Because the couple felt called to adopt a child of that age, they were eager to do everything they could to find a match. So, publishing an ad got the green light. I helped them draft a short ad and arranged for it to run in the newspaper on several occasions. Unfortunately, but not unexpectedly, I never received any response to the ad.

Time passed. In fact, a couple of years elapsed. But then one day, our office got a call from a birth mother desiring to place her two-year-old son. Did we even have a couple who might be interested since almost everyone wants to adopt a newborn? Oh, yes! The nice couple who ran the ad sometime back. We contacted them with information on the situation, and they were interested and wanted to proceed.

In looking through the prospective adoptive parents' file to prepare the required paperwork, I saw something that simply took my breath away. A copy of the ad we ran in the newspaper for them bore the publication date. The date the ad first ran was the date on which the little boy had been born!

Of course, I shared this mind-blowing fact with the couple. They had long prayed for a child to adopt and viewed this information as evidence God had answered their prayers. And, unbeknownst to them, He answered in the affirmative two years before they knew about His response. To emphasize this timing, God threw in the date of birth coinciding with the running of their ad. What awesome and sweet confirmation! They asked and God answered.

Faith Lesson

> *Before they call I will answer;*
> *while they are still speaking I will hear.*
> —Isaiah 65:24

Mentioning the word *prayer* evokes a mental picture of people asking God for something for themselves or for another. Since prayer is a two-way communication with God, the one making the request expects a response from God. Typically, they desire an immediate response and fulfillment. Heal my child today. Provide me with a job this week.

But answer and fulfillment are two separate concepts. For example, a child might ask his parents for a bike. In their minds they say yes, but they'll wait until the child's birthday or Christmas to gift him the bike. Conversely, the parents decide no, they can't afford a bike for their child. The answer is immediate, but the request's fulfillment never happens.

Our heavenly Father operates in the same way. He hears the requests believers make of Him and will always answer. Fulfillment of the request, though, won't occur if the answer is no. But even if the answer is yes, some time may elapse before its fulfillment. In the Bible, Old Testament prophecies foretold of the coming of the Messiah. The Jews asked God to send Him, but generations passed before Jesus appeared on earth. The answer was yes, but the fulfillment took place down the road.

My adventure with the adoption of the two-year-old beautifully illustrates this concept. God answered the prayers of that couple with a yes back when they started their adoption journey. But the fulfillment came some two years later. And the timing of the classified ad's publication coinciding with the child's birth confirms the contemporaneous answer God gave.

Lesson Learned: Just because you don't see it yet doesn't mean God hasn't answered your prayer.

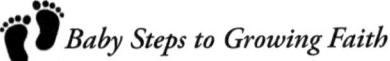
Baby Steps to Growing Faith

1. Can God answer your prayer without you having tangible proof of it?

2. What timing do you expect for an answer when you ask God for something? How about the timing for His fulfilling your request? Can the timing be different for each?

3. Does the saying "timing is everything" apply to God fulfilling a request He's answered with a yes? Why or why not?

4. Read Psalm 27:14. What does this verse tell you about God's timing?

Adventure 40

Be Prepared

Since I placed infants for adoption directly from the hospital, the most common place for a birth mother to sign a consent with me was at the hospital. This location meant I didn't have the convenience of my office where a copier, stapler, and supply closet with extra pens were handy. When I traveled outside the office to get adoption paperwork signed, it was crucial to take everything I would need with me.

Although I always had to be prepared, I also had to be flexible. Why? Circumstances, and even locations, could change at a moment's notice. I set out from my office one morning thinking my destination would be the hospital in another city. But while driving on the interstate, I spoke with the birth mother by phone. She told me she just wasn't ready to sign the paperwork and asked me to come to the hospital later in the day. Plan B arranged, I turned the car around and headed back to the office.

But before making it to the office, I received a call from the birth mother. She had now left the hospital and wanted to know if I could meet her at her parents' house just outside the city where the hospital was located. Plan C was now in effect. So, I turned the car back around and retraced my path out of town. Fortunately, no further letters of the alphabet needed to be called upon for subsequent plans.

Arriving at the home of the birth mother's parents, I was ushered into the dining room where the paperwork would be signed. I began setting up for the event, including directing who should sit where. The documents to be signed were placed on the table in a neat stack in the order in which they'd be signed. I set my notary seal close by and handed out the pens I'd brought with me. One pen for me, one for the birth mother, and one for each of the two required witnesses. I was organized and prepared. Or was I?

After identifying the first document to the birth mother, I handed the paper to her for signature. Having reviewed copies of the documents in advance, she was comfortable with them and had no questions. I pointed to the line where she should sign and reminded her to sign her name exactly as it appeared under the signature line.

Then the trouble started. The birth mother's pen wouldn't write. I tried doodling with it on a piece of scratch paper, but it didn't make a mark. "Don't worry," I said smiling. "You and I can share a pen." But my pen, which I had handed to her, wouldn't write either.

Good grief! This poor birth mother just wants to get the paperwork done and over with and these pens won't write.

One of the two witnesses kindly offered their pen to the birth mother. But, you guessed it, that pen wouldn't write either. And to add to the fun, neither would the pen I'd given to the second witness. The situation would've been funny if the nature of the paperwork hadn't been so serious. The birth mother had only been out of the hospital for a handful of hours and was eager to put the legal steps behind her to place her child for adoption.

The birth mother's parents, who'd so far maintained their composure, jumped up and hastily set off to find a pen or two somewhere in their house. I heard drawers opening and closing, and footsteps sounding in various locations in the house.

How can there be no working pens anywhere when important papers must be signed? I fumed.

Finally, the girl's mom and dad returned triumphantly with a couple of pens. To make sure all was good, I doodled with them on the back of a piece of paper. Everyone breathed a sigh of relief, and we proceeded to get the adoption paperwork signed. And no one complained about having to share a pen.

This situation led to a change in my SOP (standard operating procedure). Never again did I leave my office to get paperwork signed at another location without doodling with every single pen I was taking with me to make sure it worked.

Faith Lesson

> *At midnight the cry rang out: "Here's the bridegroom!*
> *Come out to meet him!"*
> *Then all the virgins woke up and trimmed their lamps.*
> *The foolish ones said to the wise, "Give us some of your oil;*
> *our lamps are going out."*
>
> —Matthew 25:6–8

"Be Prepared" is the motto of the Boy Scouts. Their founder, Robert Baden-Powell, explained that the words mean always being in a state of readiness.[10] Scouts should always be ready to do their duty. Regular meetings and activities train and equip the boys to live up to their motto.

Jesus also wanted His followers to be prepared. He illustrated this point in the parable of the ten virgins. While all the girls in His story possessed a lamp, the five foolish ones didn't have sufficient oil to maintain their lights. They mistakenly believed they were ready for the bridegroom's arrival and were consequently left out of the festivities.

In my pen adventure, I was seemingly prepared to have the birth mother sign legal paperwork. But I wasn't prepared sufficiently. To be truly prepared, I should have double-checked to make sure the writing instruments were in working order before I left my office.

While owning a Bible is wonderful, that fact alone doesn't make us ready for Jesus to return. Have we read it? Implemented the advice it gives? Learned all we can about the One we're waiting to meet? There's a reason the Good Book is referred to as "Basic Instructions Before Leaving Earth." Be prepared by reading rather than simply owning it.

Lesson Learned: I need to be prepared for Jesus's return.

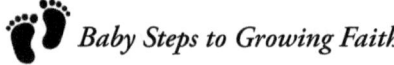
Baby Steps to Growing Faith

1. In general, what does being prepared mean to you?

---

10 Bryan Wendell, "Be Prepared: The Origin Story Behind the Scout Motto," Aaron on Scouting, May 8, 2017, https://blog.scoutingmagazine.org/2017/05/08/be-prepared-scout-motto-origin/.

2. Read the story of the virgins with the lamps found in Matthew 25:1–13. Based on Jesus's own teaching, do you think He expects you to be prepared and awaiting His second coming?

3. Would you describe yourself as "wise" or "foolish" based on your extent of preparation at this point? Why?

4. Identify one specific thing you could do today to prepare for Jesus's return. Then do it!

Acknowledgments

The first and biggest thank-you must go to my heavenly Father. He placed me where He wanted me to be: in a law office handling adoption cases. Three and a half decades later, I began a new chapter in my life using the writing abilities that He bestowed on me. And there's no more perfect topic to write about than the faith lessons He taught me through my adoption experiences. I was blessed to learn those lessons and am doubly blessed to be given the opportunity to share them with others through my words in this book.

Although I am the author, other writers poured into my effort to write this book. I tip my hat to fellow members of the Destin Chapter of Word Weavers International. These friends have offered constructive critique, moral support, and, most importantly, their heartfelt prayers for writing guidance and success.

I literally dreamed about writing this book for years. My good friend and fellow writer Felicia Ferguson stood by my side during this process, even if she did move all the way to Denver, Colorado, before I received a book contract. I appreciate her encouragement, advice, and listening ears. And let's not forget her reviewing my book proposal, which led to a book offer from Iron Stream.

Thanks also to fellow Iron Stream Media author Gretchen Huesmann. She provided hugs, encouragement, information, critique, and prayer support.

Professional editor, and even more importantly my friend, Hope Bolinger Soto proved true to her name. She imbued me with hope by taking on my book proposal as a project, providing spot-on advice, and telling me my writing was solid. I knew that if she believed in me, I really had a shot at getting my creative baby birthed.

The title *God Adopted Us First* came to me from Mike Logan, the big brother I never had, friend, Word Weaver, and title creator extraordinaire. He still keeps me in stitches all the way from Kentucky, where he now lives.

I'd be remiss without acknowledging all those with whom I interacted during my adoption practice, including attorneys, judges, court clerks, counselors, social workers, pregnant women, hospital staff, prospective adoptive parents, birth/legal/alleged fathers, adoptees, and coworkers. Each of these individuals shared a portion of my journey, helped shape my perspective of adoption, and added to what I learned about it. Without them, there would be no stories to tell.

Last, but definitely not least, is my amazing husband, John. What a wonderful sense of humor God had to bring me a husband who's an adoptee. Thank you for being there by my side not only while I wrote this book but also for doing life with me.

About the Author

For thirty-five years Alice H. Murray practiced law as a Florida adoption attorney. She concentrated on cases involving domestic, nonrelative infant adoptions.

Alice now pursues a different path. With a passion for writing, she is constantly creating with words. Her first book, *The Secret of Chimneys*, an annotated Agatha Christie mystery, was released in April 2023.

Alice's résumé includes contributions to several compilation works such as Short And Sweet books, *Chicken Soup for the Soul*, *Abba's Lessons*, and *42 Stories Anthology*. Alice is a regular contributor to *GO!*, a quarterly Christian magazine in the Florida Panhandle, and she has three devotions a month published online by Dynamic Women in Missions. Her devotions have also appeared in compilation devotionals such as *The Upper Room*, *Ordinary People Extraordinary God* (July 2023), *Guideposts's Pray a Word a Day*, Vol. 2 (June 2023), and *Pray a Word for Hope* (September 2023). On a weekly basis, Alice, as WONDER-ing Woman, posts a blog about current events with a humorous point of view and posts a faith column, *Feet To Faith*, on patheos.com.

In addition to her writing, Alice produces a weekly spot, "Murray's Motivational Moments," on digital radio station Christian Mix 106. She loves meeting with book clubs in costume either in person or via Zoom to discuss her Agatha Christie annotation. She's also taught and spoken at writers conferences.

Alice enjoys connecting with her readers. Look for her online in the following places:

Facebook: https://www.facebook.com/alicemurraywriter/
Blog: aliceinwonderingland.wordpress.com
Author website: authoralicehmurray.wixsite.com/website
Instagram: alice.h.murray
Pinterest: https://www.pinterest.com/pstyre/
X (formerly Twitter): @AliceHMurr51316
Patheos: https://www.patheos.com/blogs/feettofaith/author/amurray/

www.ingramcontent.com/pod-product-compliance
Lightning Source LLC
Chambersburg PA
CBHW060515090426
42735CB00011B/2230